American Catholics Today

American Catholics Today

New Realities of Their Faith and Their Church

William V. D'Antonio, James D. Davidson,
Dean R. Hoge, and Mary L. Gautier

A SHEED & WARD BOOK

ROWMAN & LITTLEFIELD PUBLISHERS, INC.
Lanham • Boulder • New York • Toronto • Plymouth, UK

ROWMAN & LITTLEFIELD PUBLISHERS, INC.

A Sheed & Ward Book
Published in the United States of America
by Rowman & Littlefield Publishers, Inc.

A wholly owned subsidiary of The Rowman & Littlefield Publishing Group, Inc.
4501 Forbes Boulevard, Suite 200, Lanham, Maryland 20706
www.rowmanlittlefield.com

Estover Road, Plymouth PL6 7PY
United Kingdom

British Library Cataloguing in Publication Information Available

Library of Congress Cataloging-in-Publication Data

American Catholics today : new realities of their faith and their church /
William V. D'Antonio . . . [et al.].
   p. cm.
"A Sheed & Ward book."
Includes bibliographical references and index.
ISBN-13: 978-0-7425-5214-2 (cloth : alk. paper)
ISBN-10: 0-7425-5214-4 (cloth : alk. paper)
ISBN-13: 978-0-7425-5215-9 (pbk. : alk. paper)
ISBN-10: 0-7425-5215-2 (pbk. : alk. paper)
   1. Catholic Church—History—1965– I. D'Antonio, William V.
BX1390.A46   2007
282'.73090511—dc22
                      2006037992

Printed in the United States of America

⊚ ™The paper used in this publication meets the minimum requirements of
American National Standard for Information Sciences—Permanence of Paper for
Printed Library Materials, ANSI/NISO Z39.48-1992.

Contents

Foreword

Any bishop or priest in contact with his people today knows that Catholics are not all of one cloth. They think, act, and feel differently about their faith. When asked what religion they practice, they identify themselves as Catholics, but exactly what they mean by "Catholic" varies widely.

American Catholics Today: New Realities of Their Faith and Their Church presents data that will help anyone involved in ministry in the Catholic Church to see more clearly the reality that challenges pastoral leaders at this time in the United States. Beyond the presentation of the data, moreover, the authors also offer a variety of comments on how the Church might better foster the identity and commitment of Catholics.

Some of the findings and comments might irritate, anger, or confuse some. Like any sociological analysis and survey, there is a margin of error. But don't kill the messenger: the Catholic Church in the United States lives the experience the data describe. Of course, one must distinguish the data from the comments. I hope all readers will add their own commentary to the data.

As I read the findings presented here, I found myself saying, "Yes, yes, yes!" The findings reflect what I have been experiencing over nearly forty-one years of my ministry as a priest and bishop. I also found myself being excited about talking with our staff at the Pastoral Center and with the priests, religious, deacons, and laity of our diocese about how together we can address faithfully what we know.

For too long as a Church, I think we have been tired and unimaginative in responding to the reality that is happening around us. We have struggled, too frequently unsuccessfully, to articulate in a convincing way the truths of our faith and the attitude that we, as believers, take toward the Truth. As we seek to invite deeper commitment, we need to keep in mind that in our

Catholic understanding, Church doctrine is discerned or determined not by sociological methods but by the *magisterium* in fidelity to Christ's teaching.

We can ignite the faith if we stop fighting one another and put our energies into listening and responding to God's people, who are as hungry as ever for the gospel. We can ignite the faith if as religious leaders we open ourselves more fully to God's grace and live more faithfully the gospel message. We can ignite the faith—and be ourselves ignited—if we invite, exhort, and make room for greater lay participation in the Church.

My hope is that pastoral leaders who read this book will be provoked and encouraged to be more engaged, more creative, more attentive with the laity they serve—and to pray to God more for help.

Most Reverend Gerald F. Kicanas, Bishop of Tucson

Acknowledgments

This book is the fourth in a series of studies of American Catholics. The first two were made possible by the generous financial support of the *National Catholic Reporter*, which also published special supplements of our initial findings. NCR continued to provide additional financial support for the two most recent surveys, and helped publicize these surveys with attractive supplements (the most recent on September 30, 2005). We are grateful to their publisher and editor, Sr. Rita Larivee SSA and Tom Roberts, for their continued support and help in making our surveys available to their readers. The Louisville Institute provided the major grant for the 1999 survey, and for this fourth survey they matched a grant from an anonymous donor. We are especially grateful to Dr. James Lewis and the Louisville Institute for their continued support of our surveys. We also want to thank Dr. John Cavadini, head of the theology department and director of the Institute for Church Life (ICL) at the University of Notre Dame, for his leadership in the project that led to the 2003 survey that became an important part of this book.

We wish to thank Mr. John McNee and the technical support staff of the Gallup Organization for their help in working with us to get our survey questionnaire into the proper telephone interview format, for carrying out the survey, and getting the results to us in good time. The Center for Applied Research in the Apostolate (CARA) at Georgetown University also provided data from their archives for parts of several chapters. We thank the *National Catholic Reporter* and Paul Haring for use of the picture inset of Catholics at Sunday Mass that appeared in the NCR of September 30, 2005. Valuable research and technical assistance were provided by the following: Ann Kasprzyk, Azeb Berhane, Todd Scribner, and Mary Anne Eley. Betty Seaver provided an editorial overview of each of our four volumes, and in doing so has helped smooth out the writing styles, for which we continue to be grateful

We thank Ross Miller of Rowman & Littlefield Publishers, Inc., for his enthusiastic support of our research on American Catholics, his commitment to moving our manuscript along to production, and especially for his help in all phases of the production process. Within the editorial offices of R&L, we have enjoyed working with Sarah Johnson, Ruth Gilbert, and Katherine Macdonald, each of whom has helped move the book along. Their friendly and patient style has been greatly appreciated by the four of us. And we thank the Most Reverend Gerald F. Kicanas, bishop of Tucson and Episcopal moderator for the National Association for Lay Ministry, for writing the Foreword in which he pointed to the importance of our research to the Catholic community.

Finally, we thank our families for their patience and forbearance during the year we labored to provide an accurate study of *American Catholics Today*.

1

Introduction: Catholic Laity, Catholic Faith, and the Catholic Church

We would like you to meet two women: a sixty-eight-year-old Catholic woman and her thirty-five-year-old daughter. The mother was born and raised in the Church and has been a faithful Catholic all of her life—attending Mass every week, praying the rosary regularly, accepting almost all of the Church's teachings, and contributing generously to the Church. Her daughter was baptized in the Church, attended Confraternity of Christian Doctrine (CCD) classes during her childhood, and now thinks of herself as a Catholic. She knows the basic truths of the Catholic faith and agrees with them. She says she is spiritual and has a close relationship with God, but she disagrees with the Church's opposition to artificial birth control and believes that women should be allowed to be priests. She is not registered in a parish and attends Mass only on special occasions.

The mother lives on the north side the city. The daughter lives on the south side, about twenty miles distant. Every couple of weeks, they get together for coffee and a chance to catch up on things. One day they were sitting in Starbucks, and in the course of their conversation, the subject of religion came up. The two women acknowledged that they are both Catholic and that they are of one mind on some basic issues but admitted that they have different views on a number of other things. For example, the mother—a lifelong member of her parish—can't understand why her daughter doesn't take her faith more seriously and get more involved in the Church. "After all," the mother said, "We're Catholics, and our faith and the Church should be important to us."

The daughter paused for a moment, then replied, "I don't agree with that,

1

Mom. I know we're Catholic, but the faith and the Church don't mean the same thing to me that they do to you. I believe in God, but I disagree with some parts of the faith and lots of the things the Church says or does."

How many Catholics think like the mother in our story? Like the daughter? To answer these questions, we need data on what a representative sample of American Catholics think. Second, does the conversation simply reflect differences of opinion between two people who have different views of what it means to be Catholic? Or does it point to a growing separation between the laity, their faith, and their Church? To answer these questions, we would need to know more about the way factors such as generation affect Catholic identity and the laity's commitment to the Church. Finally, do the mother/daughter differences regarding the faith and the Church lead to other differences? Do people who strongly identify with the faith and the Church (like the mother) and those who do not (like the daughter) also disagree on matters of faith and morals—on ecclesial issues such as leadership in the Church and on social issues such as the death penalty? To address these questions, we need to examine the empirical links, if any, between identity and commitment on the one hand and specific issues such as these on the other.

This book explores these questions. We use a combination of sociological theory and national surveys to describe how Catholics think about their faith and the Church, to explain why Catholics have different ways of thinking about these topics, and to understand how their thoughts about the faith and the Church affect their views on other issues. This chapter is the first step on our journey. We begin by reviewing what we have learned—and not learned—about the faith and the Church from our previous studies of American Catholics. Then we outline the approach we have used in our 2005 survey. We conclude with an overview of the remaining chapters in the book.

WHAT WE HAVE LEARNED FROM
OUR PREVIOUS STUDIES

We have explored some (but not all) of these questions in each of three previous studies: the first in 1987, the second in 1993, and the third in 1999.

The 1987 Study

As we designed our first national survey in spring 1987, Pope John Paul II was planning his second visit to the United States. In that context, we thought our survey should explore issues that would be of interest to the

Vatican and American Church leaders, both clergy and lay. The issues in 1987 had more to do with Catholics' views of the Church than with their faith. Although we collected data on the laity's demographic characteristics and their views of what it means to be a good Catholic, our focus was on Church-related topics:

- Perceptions of the Church leaders' claims to moral authority on sexual issues
- Perceptions of the laity's right to participate in Church governance
- Attitudes and beliefs about the role of women in the Church
- Financial contributions to the Church
- The laity's response to the peace and economy pastorals

The findings from the survey were summarized in the September 11, 1987, issue of the *National Catholic Reporter* and later in the book *American Catholic Laity in a Changing Church* (D'Antonio et al. 1989). We found the following:

- A laity rapidly moving from immigrant status with little education and low-paying jobs to lower-middle- and middle-class status as their education, occupation, and income moved them steadily toward mainstream America. In the process, the laity were also changing their views of the faith and the Church.
- A rather nuanced attitude about what it meant to be a "good Catholic" in matters ranging from acceptance of the pope's infallibility as teacher to attendance at Sunday Mass.
- Divided opinion about the degree to which laypeople felt the locus of moral authority on sexual matters rested solely with the bishops.
- Strong support for laity's right to participate in Church decision making.
- Strong support for an expanding role for women in the Church.
- A link between Church teachings on moral and ecclesial issues on the one hand and financial contributions to the Church on the other.
- Strong support for the pastoral letters and for the process by which they were written, especially the lay participation from both sides of the ideological spectrum.

The 1993 Study

Six years later, we thought it was time for a follow-up study. By then it was clear that Pope John Paul II wanted to restore order in what he perceived as a rather disorderly Church. *Ex Corde Ecclesiae*, the pope's vision of Catholic colleges and universities, had been published in 1990. In that document, the pope said that Catholic professors of theology should receive a letter of approval (*mandatum*) from their bishops. It was clear from the fiery response to that document that there were some—perhaps many—who disagreed with the pope's goal of tightening the reins in the Church. In the United States, the bishops' attempt to write a pastoral letter on women in the Church ended in failure in 1992. As we planned our 1993 study, our focus continued to be on the Church, with increased attention to the divisions within it. We concentrated on four issues:

- The locus of moral authority (the magisterium, individual conscience, or both)
- The gap between Church teachings and the laity's views on human sexuality
- Women's role in the Church
- Emerging issues in parish life

We also examined the way several groups of Catholics viewed issues of faith and Church, such as the "integrationists" and the "restorationists," the old and young, the highly committed versus the less committed, and Anglos versus Hispanics. As we reported in the October 8, 1993, issue of the *National Catholic Reporter* and our second book, *Laity American and Catholic: Transforming the Church* (D'Antonio et al. 1996), trends from 1987 to 1993 showed that American Catholics were moving toward an integrationist view more than a restorationist view of the faith and the Church, that generational differences were large, that integrationist views were increasingly common among the most highly committed Catholics, and that Anglo and Hispanic views on these issues were more similar than different.

The 1999 Study

Because the first two studies had been done six years apart and had produced many important results, we saw value in continuing the series six years later in 1999. As we considered what to ask in the 1999 survey, we were struck by how dramatically the Church had been changing in recent years. Pope John Paul's attempt to restore orthodoxy continued with the publication of the English version of the *Catechism of the Catholic Church* in 1999, but U.S. Catholics seemed more inclined to follow their individual consciences than to comply with Vatican norms. We noted some of these changes in the October 29, 1999, issue of the *National Catholic Reporter* and expanded on them in the book *American Catholics: Gender, Generation, and Commitment* (D'Antonio et al. 2001). Then we explored the implications these changes were having for the following:

- Catholic identity
- Participation in the sacraments and devotions
- The locus of moral authority, especially in relation to human sexuality
- The laity's views of the Church's social teachings
- The growing shortage of priests and what to do about it
- Decision making in the Church

We compared the way men and women, different generations, and Catholics who varied in commitment viewed these issues. Our findings pointed to an increasing emphasis on personal autonomy and declining levels of participation in the Catholic community. These trends were most pronounced among men, young adults, and laity who were low in commitment. However, they also were found to a lesser extent among women, the older generation, and highly committed Catholics.

THE PRESENT SITUATION

Questions about the laity's relationship to the faith and the Church seem even more urgent today. In the past half century, the Church has had four very different popes: John XXIII (1958–1963), Paul VI (1963–1978), John Paul I (1978), and John Paul II (1978–2005). They all addressed the relationship between tradition and reform, although in quite different ways. John XXIII was the most reform minded, convoking Vatican II with the goal of modernizing the Church. In the wake of Vatican II, we witnessed conflict between theological liberals and conservatives who have dramatically different views of the faith and the Church. In addition, since our 1999 survey, several other developments have rocked the Church. The encyclical *Dominus Iesus* sparked controversy on its publication in 2000. The divisions surrounding *Ex Corde Ecclesiae*'s call for a bishop's approval for theologians (*mandatum*) deepened in 2001. In 2002, the sexual abuse and leadership crisis erupted into what some describe as the most traumatic event in American Catholic history (Dolan 2002). In 2004, there was a heated debate over the role of religion in politics (Should a politician's religious affiliation determine his or her stance on political issues?) and the role of politics in religion (Should bishops deny a Catholic access to the Eucharist because of his or her views on political issues?). And in 2005, we experienced the death of Pope John Paul II—the most tradition minded of the recent popes. In the process of apostolic succession, we also witnessed the elevation of Cardinal Ratzinger to Pope Benedict XVI.

Wondering if these developments and controversies had affected Catholics' views of the faith and their views of the Catholic Church, we asked ourselves three sets of questions:

1. How important is the faith to today's Catholics, and how attached are they to the Church? To what extent and in what ways do Catholics identify with the Catholic faith? How do Catholics view the boundaries between Catholicism and other religious groups, such as the uniqueness of Catholicism and the similarity between it and other faiths? How committed are Catholics to the Church?

2. Assuming that many Catholics hold views like the mother in our story and that many others would agree with the daughter, how can we explain such differences? To what extent do the differences point to a trend? How much of the variation is due to other demographic factors, such as race, class, and gender?

3. How do Catholic identity and commitment to the Church affect Catholics' views on other issues? For example, how do they affect Catholics' views of the sacraments, the problems facing the Church today, the teaching authority of the Church, the questions of leadership and decision making in parishes, moral and political issues, and Catholic education?

We found that we were not the only people asking these questions. As we met clergy and lay leaders in meetings and as we read Catholic publications, we learned that many other people were asking essentially the same questions. They also told us that the answers would have important implications for clergy and lay leaders engaged in program planning and implementation. We found broad-based concern about the future of the faith and the Church and agreement that further research could shed light on that future.

THE 2005 STUDY

A new survey would allow us to see if there was a change in the connections between the laity, their faith, and the Church. It would also allow us to assess the effects of the sexual abuse scandal and of the recent controversies surrounding politicians' access to Catholic sacraments depending on their stands on political issues.

As in our previous studies, we sought and obtained funding from multiple sources. The Louisville Institute had contributed to our research in 1999, so we approached it again. The Institute was helpful, providing half the funds we needed. We received the other half from an anonymous foundation. We received some financial support from the *National Catholic Reporter*, which also agreed again to publish a special supplement based on our findings. For the fourth time, we hired the Gallup organization, which used an identical research process—random digit dialing—to produce a random sample of 875 self-identified American Catholics.

A Profile of Our Respondents

Our 2005 survey included questions about the respondents' race and ethnicity (to enable comparison of Anglos and Hispanics) and gender (to compare men and women). In addition, we divided the Catholic population into four generations: the pre–Vatican II generation (those born in 1940 or earlier), the Vatican II generation (those born between 1941 and 1960), the post–Vatican II generation (those born between 1961 and 1978), and the youngest generation, which we introduced for the first time in 2005 with the name "Millennials" (those born between 1979 to 1987). Because nationwide polls include respondents eighteen or older, the Millennials in 2005 are between eighteen and twenty-six years of age. We recognize that the Millennials in our study are a rather small sample of people and that young adults' religious commitments are relatively open to change. Thus, we interpret any findings about the Millennials with caution. When we compare generations from survey to survey, we compare groups of people born at the same time—not people *at the same age when being surveyed.* For example, the post–Vatican II generation averages six years older each time it is surveyed.

In addition, we collected information on marital status (married, living as married, single, or "other"), amount of education (from less than high school to graduate or professional degree), amount of Catholic schooling (none to thirteen years or more), political affiliation (Republican, Democrat, or Independent), and income (less than $25,000 to more than $100,000).

Table 1.1 provides a demographic profile of our respondents. Eighty-four percent are white, and 16 percent are people of color.[1] One-sixth of our respondents identify as Hispanic. As in most telephone surveys, our sample includes more women (54 percent) than men (46 percent). The post–Vatican II generation (40 percent) and the Vatican II generation (35 percent) are the largest. Fifty-five percent have at least one year of Catholic schooling; 8 percent have thirteen years or more. Forty-seven percent have incomes between $25,000 and $74,999. In terms of political affiliation, they are most likely to be Democrat (42 percent), followed by Republican (39 percent) and independent or other (19 percent). Two-thirds are married, 15 percent have never been married, and the others are widowed, separated, divorced, or living together as if they were married.

---

1. The 16 percent includes African Americans, Asian Americans, Native Americans, and Hispanics who see themselves as other than white.

Table 1.1. Characteristics of Respondents, 2005

	%
Race	
White	84
People of color or other	16
Ethnicity	
Hispanic	15
Non-Hispanic	85
Gender	
Men	46
Women	54
Generation	
Pre–Vatican II	17
Vatican II	35
Post–Vatican II	40
Millennial	9
Marital status	
Married	70
Living as married	3
Never married	15
Widowed	5
Separated or divorced	6
Catholic education	
None	45
1–6 years	20
7–12 years	27
13 or more years	8
Income	
Less than $25,000	10
$25,000–$49,999	24
$50,000–$74,999	23
$75,000–$99,999	19
$100,000 or more	18
Don't know or refused	6
Political party	
Democrat	42
Republican	39
Independent or other	19

An Added Feature: The 2003 Study

We were fortunate to have access to a national study that Hoge and Davidson had done for the University of Notre Dame in 2003. That survey, conducted by Princeton Survey Research Associates, included a random sample of 1,115 self-identified Catholics. It had much in common with our previous surveys, especially its questions on Catholics' identification with the faith, their attachment to the Church, their religious beliefs and practices, and their demographic characteristics. However, it also examined a number of issues that had not been included in our previous studies and that could not be explored in our new one—such as the laity's perceptions of problems in the Church and perceptions of the Catholic Church relative to other faiths. The broad outlines of the Notre Dame study have been reported in *Commonweal* magazine (Davidson and Hoge 2004), but many findings had not yet been reported. Combining the 2003 survey with our new survey allows us to say even more about the faith, the Church, and the relationship between the two, so we are using both surveys as the basis for this book. Which survey produced the various findings is clearly indicated in the title of any data table in the text and appendices.

Other Studies

In addition to the 1987, 1993, 1999, 2003, and 2005 national surveys that are the basis of this book, we include some data from several pertinent studies: William D'Antonio coauthored *The Catholic Experience of Small Christian Communities* (2000) with Bernard Lee. James Davidson and several colleagues did a national study in 1995 and, on the basis of that survey, produced the award-winning *Search for Common Ground* (1997). Davidson also collaborated on *Lay Ministers and Their Spiritual Practices* (2003). In addition, Hoge and his colleagues have carried out a series of studies on Church leadership and the Catholic priesthood (Hoge 2002; Hoge and Wenger 2003). Mary Gautier coauthored two volumes summarizing trends in American Catholicism and global Catholicism (Froehle and Gautier 2000, 2003). Gautier and her colleagues at the Center for Applied Research on the Apostolate (CARA) also have published the National Parish Inventory (Gautier and Perl 2000) and produced a number of polls of U.S. Catholics.

AN OVERVIEW

Having access to such good data, we set out first to describe Catholics' identification with their faith and their commitment to the Church. Our second goal was to explore trends and variations in the way Catholics think about these matters. Our third goal was to see how these identifications relate to Catholics' religious beliefs and practices. Hence, we put people's identification with the Catholic faith and the Catholic Church at the center of our thinking. They are a function of prior influences and the source of specific attitudes and actions. Figure 1.1 describes the lines of influence we want to assess.

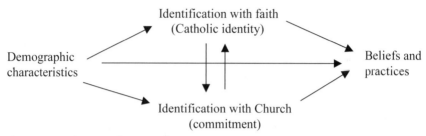

Figure 1.1. Theoretical Perspective

Describing Identity and Commitment

We asked Catholics a number of questions about their Catholic identity that probed the salience of being Catholic and how they think of Catholicism in relation to other faiths. Three items were used to measure the strength of Catholic identity: "Being Catholic is a very important part of who you are," "It is important to you that younger generations of your family grow up as Catholics," and "You can't imagine yourself being anything but Catholic." The responses were highly correlated ($r = .50$ to $.59$), forming a good index. It had a mean score of 3.93 (on a scale ranging from 1 [strongly disagree] to 5 [strongly agree]).

We measured commitment to the Church using three items that we had used for the same purpose in our 1987, 1993, and 1999 studies. They asked about the importance of the Church to the respondent, whether the respondent thought he or she would ever leave the Church, and his or her frequency of Mass attendance. The three formed an index. To score "high" on the index, a person must meet three conditions: 1) say that the Church is the most important part, or among the most important parts, of his or her life; 2) score 1 or 2 on our question about the probability of not leaving the Church; and 3) attend Mass weekly or more often. To score "low," a person must meet two of the following three conditions: say that the Catholic Church is not very important at all; score 5, 6, or 7 on the question about not leaving the Church; and attend Mass seldom or never. All other response patterns indicate a "medium" level of commitment. These categorizations were used in the analyses of all four surveys.

We treat the relationship between strength of identity and commitment to the Church as an empirical question. We do not assume that they are closely linked. If the relationship is strong and positive, the results will indicate that theological beliefs have effects on the thoughts and actions of the laity. Weaker positive correlations will suggest that the creedal faith and commitment to the institutional Church tend to go hand in hand but are only loosely connected. Based on the results of our previous surveys, we expected to find that the two are loosely but positively linked. They are likely to reinforce one another but not completely. Our findings are reported in chapter 3.

Influences

We assume that variations in Catholics' identification with the faith and their commitment to the Church are rooted in a number of conditions. Chief among these is the generation (or birth cohort) to which a Catholic belongs. Figure 1.2 shows the changing generational composition of the Catholic population since our first study in 1987. In 1987, 31 percent of Catholics belonged to the pre–Vatican II generation. Nearly half (47 percent) were in the Vatican II generation, and 22 percent were post–Vatican II Catholics. Over the years, the pre-Vatican generation has dwindled to the point where it is now only 17 percent. The Vatican II generation has gone from 47 percent of the total in 1987 to just over one-third in 2005. The post–Vatican II generation grew from 22 percent in 1987 to 40 percent. The Millennial generation, which is still in its formative stage, was 9 percent of our 2005 sample. It will grow in the years to come.

Our previous studies have shown that Catholics who are born at different points in history learn to approach the faith and the Church in different ways. People in the pre–Vatican II generation identify with the faith and the Church more than do the later generations. The 2005 study provides another opportunity to unpack the relationships between generation, identity, and commitment.

Other factors, such as race, ethnicity, and gender, also shape the way Catholics think about their faith and their Church. Some of the ones we examined turned out to have relatively little impact, so they recede into the background of our analysis. Two such factors are ethnicity and Catholic schooling. As in our previous studies, we found only small differences

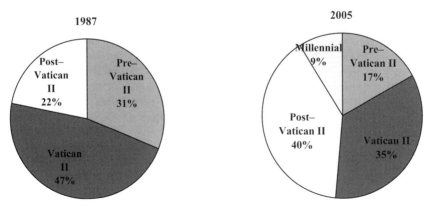

Figure 1.2. Composition of the Catholic Population by Generation, 1987 and 2005

between Hispanics and other Catholics (see appendix B). Unfortunately, we do not have enough cases to do reliable analyses of other racial and ethnic groups, such as African Americans, Asian Americans, and Native Americans. Consistent with some other research, we also found relatively few differences between Catholics who had attended Catholic schools and those who had not (see appendix A).

We also assumed that boys and girls are socialized differently with regard to religion since adult men and women have different roles in their families, the Church, and the society at large. As in our previous studies, we found some differences between males and females. Thus, gender is in the foreground of our analysis, along with generation.

Of course, people's religious identities are not simply reflections of input from others. Humans have minds of their own. They interpret the input from others, accepting some parts and rejecting some parts. In the process, they decide how important the faith and the Church will be to them personally. Accordingly, there are variations within generations, among men, and among women regarding Catholic identity and commitment to the Church.

Consequences

These variations will have consequences, as schematized in figure 1.1. Our 2005 study, like our earlier studies, shows that Catholic identity and (especially) commitment to the Catholic Church shape the way Catholics think about a range of issues, including how they think about the sacraments, the problems facing the Church, episcopal authority, leadership in the Church, and the relationship between religion and politics.

We gathered data showing trends relating to all seven of the sacraments. We also report data on Catholics' views of sacraments in general (How important are they?) and two in particular (the Eucharist and marriage). We also examine the way generation and other demographic factors, Catholic identity, and commitment affect Catholics' views of and participation in these sacraments.

Next, we use the 2003 survey to examine the importance laypeople attach to twelve problems facing the Church. Based on the laity's responses, we focused special attention on the sexual abuse crisis (How do laypeople view the actions of priests, bishops, and the media?), the priest shortage (Should the Church expand eligibility to include women and married men?), and young adults' limited participation in the Church (How involved are they?).

Another issue—episcopal authority—concerns the locus of authority on moral issues, such as abortion, birth control, divorce and remarriage, and homosexual behavior. We are able to show who Catholics believe should have the final say on such matters: Church leaders, individuals, or both. We also are able to show how these attitudes are linked to Catholic identity and commitment to the Church.

We have, as well, brand-new information on how identity and commitment affect Catholics' views on a number of leadership issues. These include the laity's views about the size of Catholic parishes (Are they too big?), parish priests (Do they expect laity to be leaders in the Church? Are they doing a good job?), the role women should play in the Church (Should they be altar servers, Eucharistic ministers, deacons, parish administrators, or priests?), ways of coping with the priest shortage (Should there be fewer masses, more foreign priests, no priests to visit the sick, no priests for last rites, or more lay parish administrators?), the laity's views on restructuring parishes (Should parishes share priests with other parishes, have more Communion services, merge parishes, or close parishes?), laypeople should be involved (decisions about parish income? diocesan income? selection of parish priests? parish closings? the ordination of women?), and the laity's role in parish finances (Should the laity play any role in such matters, have general oversight, be advisory to parish priests, or have the final say?).

We also are able to trace the connection between identity, commitment, and the laity's views on the Church's social teachings and moral/political issues such as welfare, the death penalty, abortion, and defense funding—all of which were debated during the presidential election of 2004.

As we analyze each topic, we look at how Catholics responded to each of our questions. We use cross tabulations to show how responses to one question are related to responses to another question or how scores on one index are related to scores on another. For example, we compare men and women on the Catholic Identity Index and the Church Commitment Index, and we compare how the two indices relate to each other.

THIS BOOK: AN OUTLINE

Chapter 2 examines the nature and extent of Catholic identity, including the centrality of the faith, the beliefs and practices that Catholics consider the core of the faith, and how laypeople perceive the boundaries between Catholicism and other faiths. It also shows how identity is linked to generation and other demographic characteristics. Chapter 3 explores the laity's commitment to the Church. It shows how commitment is embedded in the experiences of different generations of Catholics, and it asks about the relationship between Catholic identity and commitment to the Church. Chapter 4 examines Catholics' views of and participation in the sacraments.

Chapter 5 surveys the laity's views of what constitute the most serious problems facing the Church today. Chapter 6 explores the laity's views of episcopal authority. Chapter 7 probes issues related to church leadership. Chapter 8 examines the relationship between religion and politics. This is a new line of inquiry for us, prompted by the mixing of religion and politics in the 2004 presidential election. Chapter 9 restates our major findings and explores their implications for Church leaders.

CONCLUSION

Findings from earlier research suggest that the events of the past twenty or forty years might be widening gaps between laypersons' faith and commitment to the Church, but we needed additional data before we could draw any firm conclusions. Now we are fortunate in having data from three earlier studies (1987, 1993, and 1999) and two more recent ones (2003, 2005). As we will show, recent events have not shaken Catholics' views of the faith very much, but they have shaken Catholics' confidence in the Church. Laypeople continue to identify with the faith and remain committed to the Church, but they have many differences with the hierarchy when it comes to specific teachings and policies. Their relationship to the Church is being rethought. We are able to explain why this relationship is closer for some Catholics than others. We can also demonstrate the influence of faith and Church commitment on other religious and social issues. We begin our analysis of the unfolding story by examining the extent and nature of Catholics' identification with the faith.

2

Catholic Identity: Analysis and Trends

This chapter explores one of the two concepts at the heart of this book: identification with the Catholic faith (the other key concept—commitment to the Catholic Church—is examined in chapter 3). We examine Catholic identity in four steps. 1) We define "identity" in general and "Catholic identity" in particular, focusing on three aspects: centrality, content, and boundaries. 2) We offer a historical overview of American Catholic identity, showing how we think it has been influenced by conditions in the Church and American society in the past hundred years. 3) We use data from several national surveys to examine each of the three aspects of Catholic identity. 4) From examining the results from studies done over time and the identities of Catholics belonging to different generations, we draw several conclusions about trends in Catholic identity.

DEFINING CATHOLIC IDENTITY

In general, the term *identity* refers to a person's sense of self, his or her self-concept. Here we are especially concerned with Catholic identity, that is, the extent and nature of identification with the Catholic faith.[1]

Three Starting Points for Analysis

Individual identity is complex and is best studied from three starting points. The first looks at the aspects of life that are most important to peo-

---

1. Like other researchers who study identity, we use the terms *identity* and *self-concept* interchangeably (Rosenberg 1979; Stryker 1991; Stryker and Serpe 1994). We also distinguish Catholic identity as it is defined by the institutional Church in canon law ("official identity") and Catholic identity as it is viewed by individual Catholics ("subjective identity"). This distinction is also called *de jure* versus *de facto* identity; the latter is our primary interest here.

ple (e.g., their race, gender, and religion). This dimension of Catholic identity refers to the degree to which people identify with the Catholic faith in
relation to other identifications. In other words, how important is it to a
person to be Catholic? How salient is it? We use the term *centrality* in relation to this dimension.

The second starting point asks about the *content* of any identity (i.e., what
it means more specifically to be, e.g., black, female, or Catholic). This
dimension specifies what people consider the most important aspects of
the Catholic faith. What do people consider the core of the faith, and what
is on the periphery?

The third starting point looks at the relationship between one's identity
and other identities (e.g., the *boundaries* between being black and white,
female and male, and Catholic and Protestant). For our purposes, this
dimension has to do with people's sense of how Catholic faith relates to
other faiths. Do Catholics think that their faith is "the one true faith," or
do they think that it is no more valid or true than any other religion?

Social Contexts

Any identity is formed within three contexts: time, place, and relationships. Time has to do with the period when one was born and reared (i.e.,
the birth cohort to which one belongs). Place refers to the nation, state, or
community in which one grew up. Relationships involve interactions with
the people whom the individual considers important (i.e., one's "significant others"). Thus, to some extent, one learns or acquires an identity from
the people who are in one's social network. By extension, the more one's
network of significant others remains intact, the more likely one's identity
is to persist over time; to the extent that they change, one's identity also is
subject to change.

We are especially interested in the religious identity of four generations
of American Catholics: pre–Vatican II, Vatican II, post–Vatican II, and Millennial. The members of each generation are affected by their significant
others, including their parents and siblings, members of their extended
family, their peers, and other influential people, such as their schoolteach-
ers, religion instructors, and parish pastors. Catholics' relationships with
these people consist of multiple communications. Some are verbal (such as
when a mother tells her son that "God would be very happy with the way
you treated your sister this afternoon"). Others are nonverbal (as when a
father's warm smile clearly communicates approval of a child's behavior).
Thus, by one means or another, significant others affect the way Catholics
think about their faith. The more stable one's relationships are with significant others, the more stable one's Catholic identity is likely to be. The
more the significant others change, the more one's religious identity is subject to change.

The Individual's Role

Yet one's significant others cannot wholly determine the outcome of their efforts. Ultimately, an individual interprets the signals he or she gets from varied sources and decides the nature of his or her identity at any given time. The person also can choose to retain or alter his or her network of significant others and, in the process, modify his or her self-concept. Thus, the individual exercises some degree of "agency" in the formation and persistence of identity. For example, a young person studying piano will strengthen his or her identity as a pianist if feedback from others is positive or will weaken that identity if the feedback is negative.

The same principles apply to the individual's role in shaping his or her own Catholic identity. Significant others can affect the way laypeople identify with the Catholic faith. The signals from others may be consistent or inconsistent. If the latter, the persons must interpret the diverse input and decide which input is right or wrong, which ideas to accept or reject. In the end, they decide how important various spheres of life are, what is most important within those spheres, and how those spheres are linked to others. They also decide who is or is not included in their social networks.

Now, let us put some meat on these theoretical bones by showing how we think Catholic identity has varied across generations of American Catholics.

HISTORICAL OVERVIEW

Let us begin with the 1930s and 1940s, when Catholics, along with other Americans, experienced a severe economic depression and World War II. These times called for great sacrifice, interdependence, and respect for authority. In this period, there also was some prejudice and discrimination against Catholics by Protestants—the nation's religious insiders. Catholics, for their part, aspired to become accepted as solid Americans (Gleason 1994). The Church emphasized the importance of being Catholic; specifically, it taught Catholic doctrines such as Mary's role as the Mother of God, Christ's real presence in the Eucharist, and the belief that the Catholic Church was "the one true Church." An example is found in *The Catholic Family Handbook* of 1959, advertised as a practical guide for family life:

> Remain alert for indications that they [children in public schools] may be unduly influenced by non-Catholic thinking. In communities heavily populated by those outside the faith, Catholic children seem to be especially subject to the fallacy that "one religion is as good as another." Once this idea is accepted it is an easy step into a mixed marriage and the loss of faith. You can help counteract this influence by impressing upon your child that the Church's

unbroken line of authority extends back to St. Peter, whom Our Lord desig-
nated as the founder of His true Church. (Kelly 1959, 67)

Catholics growing up under these circumstances were in a context in which
Catholic identity was ascribed by birth and clear as a bell. Being Catholic
was a central facet of one's identity. Obeying church teachings was a given.
Seeing Catholicism as distinct from—and truer than—other faiths was a
taken-for-granted assumption.

Next, we turn to the 1950s and 1960s. In the wake of World War II,
Americans went through a period of relative prosperity (compared to the
Great Depression of the 1930s) and political tranquility (the Eisenhower
years). The Cold War united Americans against the "godless communists"
of the Soviet Union and, in the process, fostered a strong sense of patriotism. However, by the mid-1960s, the nation had shifted from tranquility
to turbulence, from patriotism to protest. Meanwhile, American Catholics
were gaining acceptance and moving up the nation's social ladder. They
also were going through another shift, this one in their Church. As a result
of Vatican II, Catholics found that their Church was opening the windows
to let in some fresh air and trying to modernize itself. For example, the
Church moved from a negative view of modern society as hostile to the
Catholic faith to a more positive view of society as God's creation. Rather
than characterizing Protestants as an enemy of the faith and emphasizing
the differences between the groups, the Church adopted a more ecumenical
attitude and pointed to areas of common ground. In the process, some
Catholics, especially members of the Vatican II generation, began to question the centrality of being Catholic, to wonder about what was the core of
the Catholic faith, and to think of the boundaries between Catholicism and
other faiths as being fairly inconsequential. In other words, Catholic identity was undergoing a change. Chester Gillis (1999) describes it:

> Most pre-Vatican II members are deeply wed to their Catholic identity. For
> them what the church teaches and what direction the American church takes
> matter, whether they agree or disagree with the direction. The church has been
> so formative in their lives that they cannot be indifferent. Many Vatican II
> Catholics are also vested in the church but are more likely to distance them-
> selves from the politics of the church. For example, they want their children
> to be Catholics, but they do not want the Catholic Church to dominate their
> children's lives the way it did theirs in their youth. The church should be part
> of their lives, not the exclusive focus. (31)

Third, we turn to the 1980s and 1990s. As the post–Vatican II generation
came into being, American society entered a period of political conserva-
tism, witnessing the end of the Cold War. By now, American Catholics were
clearly in the middle class. However, they were divided along liberal/con-

servative lines. The hierarchy was trying to restore order in what it perceived as a chaotic Church. The Catholic laypeople were becoming more autonomous in their thinking about issues of faith and morals. The post–Vatican II generation extended the previous generation's uncertainties about the centrality of being Catholic, became increasingly willing to disagree with the Church on what some viewed as optional Church teachings, and emphasized the similarities—not the differences—between Protestants and Catholics. Catholicism seemed more voluntary and less ascribed than ever.

Finally, as Americans made the transition from the twentieth century to the twenty-first, the cultural and political climate became more conservative. Catholic voices, though split, gravitated in a conservative direction. The September 11, 2001, attacks sent a jolt of national insecurity throughout the country, precipitated wars in Afghanistan and Iraq, and muted social criticism at home. Catholics, meantime, were firmly in the upper-middle class but also were becoming ever more diverse as new immigrants streamed in. And, in 2002–2003, they experienced what some consider the most traumatic episode in U.S. Catholic history—the sexual abuse scandal. As the new generation of Millennial Catholics came of age, the scandal seemed to raise new questions about the importance of being Catholic, the substance of being Catholic, and the boundaries between Catholicism and other faiths. Gillis (1999) describes the half-century of historical change:

> There is no denying that American Catholicism at the end of the twentieth century is a church marked by diversity and difference. Catholics differ with one another about authority, abortion, issues of sex and gender, social and ethical concerns, and even spirituality. They differ with the Vatican on the same issues and the more central issues of identity and control: who is the church and who should be making the rules? Fifty years ago these were not questions. Catholics thought of the church as the hierarchy and ceded virtually all authority to administer the church to the pope, bishops, and priests, in that order. The laity were the footsoldiers in the army of Christ. (5)

With this historical overview, we expect to find considerable variation in the way today's Catholics think about their faith. We also should find that these variations are linked to generation. Let's see.

CENTRALITY: THE IMPORTANCE
OF BEING CATHOLIC

The 2005 study included three items assessing the strength of Catholic identity. They are presented in table 2.1. Eighty-five percent of Catholics agreed that "being Catholic is a very important part of who you are." Seventy-eight percent said, "It is important to you that younger generations of

Table 2.1. Agreement with Three Statements about Being Catholic, 2005

	%
Being Catholic is a very important part of who you are.	85
It is important to you that younger generations of your family grow up as Catholics.	78
You can't imagine yourself being anything but Catholic.	70

your family grow up as Catholics." Finally, 70 percent agreed that "you can't imagine yourself being anything but Catholic."[2] For these people, being Catholic is quite central and important.

The responses to these items in 2005 were highly correlated with one another. In other words, responses to one tended to resemble responses to the others. Therefore, we combined them into a single index of centrality. Index scores ranged from 1 (indicating low centrality) to 5 (indicating high centrality).[3] The mean score of the index was 3.93, showing that most Catholics attach considerable importance to being Catholic. As we and other researchers have found, being Catholic is an important part of how Catholics identify themselves. For the most part, they are happy to be Catholic. They're proud to be Catholic. They like being Catholic.

Yet we also found variations. Being Catholic is more important to some people than others. How are we to explain these variations? One possible influence has to do with the period of time when Catholics were born and raised. Our historical overview suggests that there are likely to be sizable differences among the generations. As table 2.2 shows, this is the case. Older Catholics feel their Catholicism most strongly, and the youngest generation feels it the least.

Strength of Catholic identity is slightly associated with level of education in that respondents with postgraduate or professional education included a few more people scoring low than respondents with less education. Whether the respondents had attended Catholic elementary school, high

---

2. The 2003 study included three similar items. This time, 66 percent said, "I cannot imagine myself being anything other than Catholic." Sixty-three percent agreed that "there is something very special about being Catholic that you can't find in other religions." And 52 percent said, "I could be just as happy in some other church—it wouldn't have to be Catholic."

3. All three items were scored strongly agree = 5, somewhat agree = 4, don't know = 3, somewhat disagree = 2, and strongly disagree = 1. Cronbach's alpha (a measure of reliability) for the three-item index is .78. In order to study the full range, we labeled the score of 5 as "high," scores from 3.6 through 4.8 as "medium," and scores below 3.6 as "low."

Table 2.2. Strength of Catholic Identity by Generation, 2005

	Catholic Identity		
	Low %	*Medium %*	*High %*
Total Catholics	29	46	24
Pre–Vatican II	22	45	33
Vatican II	31	44	25
Post–Vatican II	27	50	24
Millennials	47	46	7

school, or college was not associated with strength of identity. European Catholics and Hispanics were similar to each other, as were men and women.

The 2003 study included two questions that approached the centrality issue in a different way (see table 2.3). The questions asked about what the respondent had learned while growing up. The responses indicate that Catholics, overall, were taught that one's personal relationship with God is more important than the importance of the institutional Catholic Church and that living a Christian way of life is more important than knowing what the Catholic Church teaches. We looked to see if backgrounds of the respondents predicted their responses, and we found that generation was a predictor: younger persons were most likely to say that they had learned more about "the importance of your personal relationship with God" than "the importance of the Catholic Church" and that they had learned more about living a Christian life than knowing what the Catholic Church teaches. Put simply, the generations differ from one another in that Catho-

Table 2.3. Two Questions Assessing Centrality of Commitments, 2003

	%
On each pair, please tell me which ONE you learned the most about while growing up—the first or the second one.	
The importance of the Catholic Church	20
The importance of your personal relationship with God	65
Both equally	13
Don't know	1
To know what the Catholic Church teaches	33
To live a Christian way of life	49
Both equally	15
Don't know	1

lic identity is not as strong among younger Catholics as it is among older ones. This finding is consistent with the results of our other surveys.

Overall level of education also was important in that among adults aged forty-two or younger, the more educated respondents said they had learned more about living a Christian way of life than about what the Catholic Church teaches. The number of years of Catholic education was a predictor for persons aged forty-three or older: the more Catholic education the respondents had received, the more they had learned about what the Catholic Church teaches as opposed to living a Christian way of life. Gender and ethnicity were not related to responses on these questions.

Another survey useful in assessing the centrality of Catholicism was done in 1996, commissioned by William D'Antonio. He designed a nationwide survey of self-identified Catholics in which he asked, "How important are [the following] to you?" (see table 2.4). Clearly in first place was the importance of family (a ranking in agreement with all other research on Americans' commitments), followed by commitments to the society ("helping other people" and "the environment"). Prayer and spiritual matters are ranked higher than the Catholic Church in general and the respondent's own parish in particular. The Catholic Church is halfway down the list. "Having nice things" and "money" are ranked lower. The most important findings for present purposes are the centrality of the family and the greater centrality of Catholic prayer and spirituality than of Catholic parish life.

Table 2.4. Importance of Key Values to American Catholics, 1996 Survey

	Very Important %
Your family	96
Helping other people	77
The environment	69
Prayer	69
Spiritual matters	60
Your job or career	58
Your particular parish or church	53
The Catholic Church	43*
Money	31
Studying the Bible	29
Political issues	26
Having nice things	15

* The figure 43 is an approximation because the available responses on this question were a bit different from those on other questions.
Source: D'Antonio et al. (1996).

CONTENT: CORE AND PERIPHERY

The second aspect of Catholic identity is understandable if we begin by asking a different question. When a person says he or she is Catholic, *what is it about* Catholicism that is important for that person? Catholicism, like all centuries-old religious traditions, encompasses an array of texts, teachings, rituals, devotions, prophets, reformers, and saints. The history is so rich with teachings and persons that no Catholic today can embrace them all, much less know them all. Each Catholic is forced to make selections, holding fast to what is spiritually authentic and treating the rest as interesting but not really crucial. Theologians call this the hierarchy of truths.

Distinguishing the essential from the nonessential is not a new problem. In America it has been a special preoccupation of Catholic thinkers because some traditional Catholic institutional norms have been at odds with American ideals. To exemplify the problem: Bishop John Ireland of Minneapolis argued in about 1900 that Catholicism in America would be greatly aided if it made some institutional adaptations to American culture. He argued that Catholics need to distinguish between the divine and the human, the essentials and the accidents:

> The divine never changes. It is of Christ, the same . . . forever. But even in the divine we must distinguish between the principle and the application of the principle. The application of the principle, or its adaptation to environment, changes with the circumstances.

Further, "the Church, while jealously guarding the essentials," should be ready "to abandon the accidentals, as circumstances of time and place demand" (cited in Dolan 2002, 101).

Church leaders need to know not only the hierarchy of truths as defined theologically but also what the laity know in their minds and hearts.[4] Put differently, what do laity today *feel* is most central, authentic, and important in being Catholic?

Our 1999 and 2005 surveys sought to learn what laity feel is central to being Catholic and what they feel is peripheral or optional. This information is important, because in times of social and cultural change, not everything in a religious tradition can be maintained unaltered from the past. Whenever there is social change, devotees of Catholicism, like devotees of any tradition, encounter the need to make selections. Catholics must decide what they must hold fast to as solid rock and what they may see as open to possible reevaluation.

The 2005 survey asked, "As a Catholic, how important is each of the following twelve elements of Catholicism to you? Would you say it is very important, somewhat important, or not important at all?" The percentage saying "very important" to each is shown in figure 2.1. Tied for first place are "Helping the poor" and "Belief in Jesus' resurrection from the dead." In third place is "The sacraments, such as the Eucharist," and closely following is "The Catholic Church's teachings about Mary as the Mother of God."

By contrast, in last place among the twelve elements was "A celibate male clergy," followed by "The Catholic Church's teachings that oppose the death penalty" and "The teaching authority claimed by the Vatican." Most

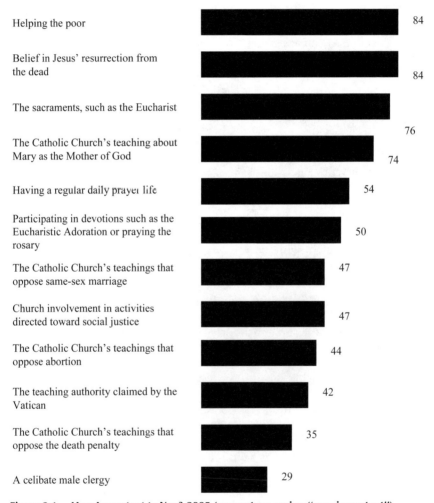

Helping the poor	84
Belief in Jesus' resurrection from the dead	84
The sacraments, such as the Eucharist	76
The Catholic Church's teaching about Mary as the Mother of God	74
Having a regular daily prayer life	54
Participating in devotions such as the Eucharistic Adoration or praying the rosary	50
The Catholic Church's teachings that oppose same-sex marriage	47
Church involvement in activities directed toward social justice	47
The Catholic Church's teachings that oppose abortion	44
The teaching authority claimed by the Vatican	42
The Catholic Church's teachings that oppose the death penalty	35
A celibate male clergy	29

Figure 2.1.   How Important to You? 2005 (percentage saying "very important")

of the questions in figure 2.1 were asked in the 1999 survey, and the results were the same. Feelings about centrality have not changed.

Millennial and post–Vatican II Catholics rated two items *much lower* than did Vatican II and pre–Vatican II Catholics: the Church's teachings on abortion and the Church's teachings on same-sex marriage. Also, more generally, the younger the Catholic, the less importance he or she gave to the Church's involvement in activities directed toward social justice. We looked to see if respondents with a history of Catholic schooling were different from others on the items in figure 2.1; they were not. What about the effects of *overall* education level, regardless of any Catholic school or college? Differences were small, except that the less educated respondents gave somewhat higher importance ratings to Catholic teachings that oppose same-sex marriage and teachings about Mary as the Mother of God. Men and women were different on three of the items: women saw daily prayer life and helping the poor as more important than did men, and men saw the Church's teachings opposing same-sex marriage as more important than did women.

The 2003 survey asked a similar series of questions: "How important are the following teachings to *your vision* of what the Catholic faith is about? Would you say essential; may or may not be essential; or not essential?" (see figure 2.2). The findings were similar to the findings in the 2005 survey in that the sacraments and charity toward the poor are at the top, and two topic areas are at the bottom—specific moral teachings and specific teachings about the priesthood. The responses varied by generation; younger Catholics generally rated the various items as less essential than did older Catholics. The greatest generational differences were that younger Catholics saw weekly Mass attendance, the belief that only men can be priests, and the belief that Jesus is really present in the Eucharist as less essential.

We also compared responses of Catholics with more Catholic education versus those with less, and we found no differences. What about the level of education in general apart from specifically Catholic education? We found a pattern in that the more educated Catholics (with a college degree or more) tended to rate many of the items as less essential than did the less educated Catholics. In particular, the more educated Catholics rated private confession to a priest and attending Mass weekly as less essential. For example, 26 percent of Catholics with a college degree rated private confession

---

4. The analysis of core versus periphery in religious traditions is common in the sociology of religion. For its use in the study of Judaism, see Cohen (1983, 26). In the Assemblies of God, see Poloma (2005, 77–79). In Protestant denominations, see Miller (1997, 155–56). The theory holds that when the core is felt by the faithful as more sacred than the periphery, the periphery is left open for adaptive experimentation, and this facilitates innovating in useful ways.

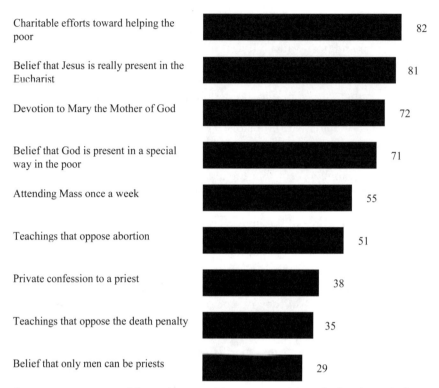

Charitable efforts toward helping the poor — 82

Belief that Jesus is really present in the Eucharist — 81

Devotion to Mary the Mother of God — 72

Belief that God is present in a special way in the poor — 71

Attending Mass once a week — 55

Teachings that oppose abortion — 51

Private confession to a priest — 38

Teachings that oppose the death penalty — 35

Belief that only men can be priests — 29

Figure 2.2.   How Essential Are These Teachings to Your Vision of What the Catholic Faith Is About? 2003 (percentage saying "essential")

to a priest as essential, compared with 52 percent of those with less than a high school diploma. When we studied the impact of educational levels within age strata, we found that the patterns were unchanged, indicating that they are not merely an artifact of age. Also men and women gave similar responses.

The findings here are similar to the findings of earlier studies asking these questions (see D'Antonio et al. 2001, 46–49). In every assessment, Catholic laity reported that sacraments and charity toward the poor were central to their understanding of Catholicism. Devotion to Mary the Mother of God was almost as central. In 2005, we asked about belief in Jesus' resurrection from the dead, and it came out highest of all. By contrast, other elements came out consistently low: specific moral teachings about the death penalty, abortion, and labor unions and specific Church rules, for example, saying that only celibate men could be priests.

BOUNDARIES: CATHOLIC DISTINCTIVENESS

The objective boundaries of Catholicism defined in official Church documents may not be the same as the boundaries that laity *feel*. Objectively, a Catholic is a person who has been baptized as a Catholic and has not explicitly abandoned Catholicism, either to join another church or to withdraw from all religion. Subjectively, such a person may not feel committed to the Catholic faith or community and thus is not subjectively Catholic. This person remains a Catholic, but his or her behavior will be different. For practical purposes, the main issue regarding subjective boundaries is around who is a "good Catholic," not merely who is "a Catholic." A "good Catholic" is objectively defined by faith, participation in the sacraments, and involvement in Catholic community life. How do laity feel about the importance of these requirements? Put differently, which boundaries do the Catholic laity believe in for themselves, and which ones do they not? Which definitions of a "good Catholic" do they accept?

Our surveys approached the issue of boundaries by saying, "The following statements deal with what you think it takes to be a good Catholic. Please tell me if you think a person can be a good Catholic without performing these actions or affirming these beliefs." Table 2.5 shows the per-

Table 2.5.   Can You Be a Good Catholic without This? Yes. 1987, 1993, 1999, and 2005 Surveys

	1987 %	1993 %	1999 %	2005 %
Without believing that Jesus physically rose from the dead.	—	—	23	23
Without believing that in the Mass, the bread and wine actually become the body and blood of Jesus.	—	—	38	36
Without donating time or money to help the poor.	44	52	56	44
Without obeying the Church hierarchy's teaching regarding abortion.	39	56	53	58
Without donating time or money to help the parish.	—	57	60	58
Without obeying the Church hierarchy's teaching on divorce and remarriage.	57	62	65	66
Without their marriage being approved by the Catholic Church.	51	61	68	67
Without obeying the Church hierarchy's teaching on birth control.	66	73	72	75
Without going to church every Sunday.	70	73	77	76

centages who said *yes* in 1987, 1993, 1999, and 2005. At the top of the table are the *most* essential requirements for being a good Catholic, and at the bottom are the *least* essential ones. The table tells us that *creedal beliefs* are the main boundary markers of the faith: belief in Jesus' resurrection and belief in the Real Presence in the Eucharist. They are more important than all the others. Next comes the obligation to donate time or money to help the poor; it is deemed more important than donating time or money to help the *parish* (fifth in the table).

At the bottom of table 2.5 are the least imperative requirements for being a good Catholic: attending church every Sunday and obeying Church teachings on birth control. Third and fourth least important are having one's marriage approved by the Catholic Church and obeying Church teachings on divorce and remarriage. In summary, creedal beliefs are seen as a crucial requirement for being a Catholic, but weekly Mass attendance and obedience to Church teachings about birth control are not.

Table 2.5 also gives us information about trends since 1987. Although not all the questions were asked in the earlier surveys, we can see that Catholics today, compared with Catholics in 1987, are less convinced of the importance of obeying Church teachings about abortion (a change of 19 percentage points) and of having their marriages approved by the Church (a change of 16 percentage points). They see slightly less importance in obeying Church teachings on divorce, remarriage, and birth control. Whether Catholics today see matters of faith as less important today is unclear because we lack data prior to 1999 on the top two items in the table.

Do young people and older people in 2005 agree on what one needs to do to be a good Catholic? Not on everything. The young adults (members of the post–Vatican II and Millennial generations) say that there are fewer requirements for being a good Catholic. The most extreme difference between young and old was on the question of obeying Church teachings on abortion. The youngest generation saw this as *much less* essential—89 percent said yes, it was okay to disobey the teachings, compared with 44 percent in the oldest generation. Attitudes about obeying teachings about birth control had a similar but smaller difference by age: 87 percent of the young said that they were unessential, compared with 61 percent in the oldest generation.

Does Catholic education make a difference? We checked and found that, on the whole, it does not. How about overall level of education, whether Catholic or not—does it influence these attitudes? Yes, on two of the items in table 2.5. The more highly educated Catholics were less insistent than the others about the requirements of obeying Church teachings on birth control and on divorce and remarriage. Men and women held similar views.

Two other items in the 2005 survey tell us about how Catholics perceive boundaries to the faith. One states, "Catholicism contains a greater share of truth than other religions do," with which 56 percent agreed. This tells us that about half of American Catholics are uncertain about the greater truth of Catholicism as a defining boundary. Older persons tended to agree more—61 percent of Catholics 65 or over did so, compared with 43 percent of those 26 or younger. Also, the less educated persons tended to agree more. Level of Catholic education and gender had no effect.

The second statement declares, "How a person lives is more important than whether he or she is a Catholic." Eighty-eight percent agreed. This tells us that the vast majority of Catholics take more seriously a person's moral behavior than his or her denominational membership. Catholic laity affirm non-Catholics who act morally. On this statement, young and old had the same attitude, as did those with more and less education, those with more and less Catholic education, and men and women.

Other Research on Catholic Boundaries

The 1983 Notre Dame Study of Catholic Parish Life asked Catholic laity a similar question (Castelli and Gremillion 1987). It is more than twenty years old, yet the findings are instructive for us. The sample for that study did not include all Catholics but only those who are registered in parishes. The survey asked, "In your judgment, should persons be considered 'true' Catholics if they . . .?" Nine types of behavior were then listed, shown in table 2.6.

The top five behaviors in the table are the ones that not many respondents said "true Catholics" could do—they are the most important boundaries. Having or urging an abortion is the most serious offense in the table

Table 2.6. Who Is a True Catholic? Survey of Catholics Registered in Parishes, 1983

"In your judgment, should persons be considered true Catholics, if they . . ."	
Yes *response*	%
Urge or undergo abortion	25
Commit "major" crimes	31
Practice homosexuality	32
Oppose racial integration	37
Live together outside marriage	37
Rarely go to Mass	50
Are married "outside" the church	55
Commit "minor" crimes	56
Oppose nuclear disarmament	72

Source: Castelli and Gremillion (1987, 50).

(the top item), followed by committing major crimes and practicing homosexuality. "Opposing racial integration" is also high in the list. This 1983 study looked solely at behaviors, not at beliefs, but we see that abortion was rated as a serious sinful behavior and missing Mass was not, just as in 2005.

In short, Catholic identity does not preclude tolerance of other faiths. Indeed, Catholics seem to value their own faith, including its distinctive qualities, while also being open-minded about the tenets of other religious traditions.

Two Boundaries to Catholicism

A recent study of mainline Protestants' perceptions of boundaries (also called "zones") offers some insights that are helpful to our analysis of Catholic boundaries. The Protestant study distinguished between two boundaries, one of which is inside the other. The wider zone is the "tolerance zone." For most mainline Protestants, most of the world's great religions—Christian and non-Christian—are in that zone. For example, groups such as Islam and Hinduism are inside the zone of tolerance. The only faiths falling outside this zone are religions that advocate violence, oppression, or rigid control of members. Whether any world religion merited tolerance was mainly a matter of morality and civility, not matters of specific theological teachings, which were usually seen by mainline Protestants as tolerable (Hoge et al. 1994).

Although the tolerance zone is broad for most mainline Protestants, for some it is smaller (including Christianity but little else). The researchers lacked precise measures to know exactly how many Protestants had a broader tolerance zone and how many had a narrower one.

The smaller of the two zones is the "personal comfort zone," which includes only the denominations in which the respondent would feel personally comfortable. For most mainline Protestants, this zone includes most Protestant denominations but not fundamentalists, Evangelicals, and Pentecostals (Hoge et al. 1994, 120).

The distinction between these zones, each with its subjective boundary, can help us understand the Catholic situation today. Based on our findings so far, we expected that Catholics—like mainline Protestants—would have a broad tolerance of other religions, both inside and outside Christianity. However, we also expected that most Catholics feel less comfortable in non-Catholic religions; that is, their personal comfort zone would be usually limited to Catholicism. We explored these hypotheses using data from our 2003 study.

The Tolerance Zone

The 2003 survey contained four statements that help us assess Catholics' tolerance of other religions, including major world religions (see table 2.7). First of all, a slight majority of Catholics claimed that "the Catholic religion contains a greater share of the truth than other religions." But, even as they professed belief in the distinctiveness of their own faith, they expressed a great deal of tolerance toward other faiths. Eighty-six percent said that "if you believe in God, it doesn't really matter which religion you belong to." Three-quarters agreed that "major world religions are equally good ways of finding ultimate truth." Just over half said that "the Catholic religion has no more spiritual truth than other major religions." Thus, as we suspected, today's Catholics have a preference for their own faith but also have a rather wide tolerance of other religious worldviews.[5]

We checked the determinants of the statements in table 2.7. Highly educated Catholics were least likely to agree that Catholicism has more truth than other religions. Younger Catholics and persons with higher education

Table 2.7.   **Statements about Catholicism and Other Religions, 2003**

	Strongly Agree or Somewhat Agree %
Catholic distinctiveness	
The Catholic religion contains a greater share of the truth than other religions do.	53
Tolerance of others	
If you believe in God, it doesn't really matter which religion you belong to.	86
The major world religions are equally good ways of finding ultimate truth.	74
The Catholic religion has no more spiritual truth than other major religions.	52

Source: ND Survey (2003)

5. We looked at nationwide poll data to see if Catholics are more or less relativistic about religious teachings than Protestants. The best data we found were from the high-quality General Social Survey in 1998. The question asked if one religion has the truth or if basic truths are in many religions. The percentages saying that "there are basic truths in many religions" were 91 for Catholics, 83 for all Protestants, 85 for mainline Protestants, and 71 for evangelical Protestants. Catholics and mainline Protestants are similar. Data are from http://sda.berkeley.edu/cgi-bin/hsda3 (accessed May 26, 2006).

were more tolerant of other groups than older and less educated Catholics were. Men and women held similar attitudes, and the effect of having had Catholic education was slight.

To help us appreciate the importance of these findings, we turn to historian Chester Gillis's contrast between pre–Vatican Catholicism and the Catholicism of the 1990s:

> Catholics protested against the Catholic "ghetto" of the 1940s and '50s and longed to be assimilated into the larger American culture. Since the 1960s they have been assimilated—to the point that many are now virtually indistinguishable from others in the society. A simultaneous consequence of this successful assimilation is the loss of group identity, lack of a common vision, detachment from specific marks of identification, and appropriation of practices and values esteemed by the common culture, whether or not they adhere to Catholic principles. (1999, 278)

The Personal Comfort Zone

For most Catholics, the personal comfort zone includes Catholicism and a few similar groups (such as Anglicanism and Lutheranism) but not much else. Our evidence is mainly from the 2003 survey, where 66 percent agreed with "I can't imagine myself being anything but Catholic" and 52 percent agreed with "I could be just as happy in some other church—it wouldn't have to be Catholic." These data suggest that Catholics' personal comfort zone seems to be a little broader than just Catholicism but not nearly as inclusive as their tolerance zone. It is wider for young adult Catholics than for older Catholics. For example, 56 percent of respondents thirty-nine years of age or younger said, "I could be just as happy in some other church," compared with 37 percent of respondents aged sixty-three or older.

Thus, we have evidence for a new understanding of religious boundaries for Catholics. The vast majority—and especially younger Catholics—are tolerant of other religions' truth claims, yet over half of all Catholics include little else in their personal comfort zone. We carried out a series of personal interviews with young adults to try to understand this new situation. Here is a typical person. Sarah is a twenty-seven-year-old graduate student in psychology. She grew up in a Catholic family and went to church and Confraternity of Christian Doctrine (CCD) for many years. She affirms her religious training:

> Sarah: I think it was tremendously worthwhile. I don't think it was a waste of time, even though my views have changed. There's a lot of things I don't believe in the Catholic Church and in the Bible, but I don't think it's ever a waste of time to give a child a base for morals, for how to act. And also just

for the sheer fact of what it brings to the family—to have something to focus on, to know that when Christmas time rolls around, it's not just Santa Claus and reindeer. It's the birth of Jesus, and this is something we celebrate and get emotional about together and it kind of brings us together. And every Sunday we do this as a family and we talk about church and we go to church and have breakfast and talk about what we learned in CCD. and all that.

Interviewer: Is Catholicism more true than any other religion, such as Islam?

Sarah: I don't think that any one religion is more true than another. I think people believe what they believe based on evidence. And I think that you can find that evidence, if you look hard enough for it. You can find it *somewhere*. And I think some of the older religions that don't follow the New Testament and don't believe in Christ, there is just as much evidence for those as there is for Christianity. I don't think any of them are any less true. I think the basics of all religions really come from the same place, and it has just sort of been taken in different directions by different groups of people.

Interviewer: What if we really wanted to know what God wants? How would we find that out?

Sarah: I'm not sure that you ever could know. I think religion and the belief in God, in and of itself is just a matter of faith. There is no evidence for that. I don't think you can prove it one way or the other. I think it's a matter of, do you believe it and how much do you believe it? . . . There's no proof that God exists or that He cares about us. It's faith. I don't think you'll ever find proof that any religion is true or any specific religious teaching is true. That's not what it's about. It's about believing and having faith and having the courage to believe it in the face of not having any evidence. . . . I'm not sure where, exactly, to find God's will. I think when things go well and people treat each other properly and treat themselves properly, I think that's God's will.

Interviewer: You said you continue to be Catholic. That is your choice. You don't *have* to be Catholic.

Sarah: Right. It's because it brings an element to my life that is necessary and important. It's not something that I can do without, something that I can just take away and say, "I'm not Catholic any more." Because I would miss out on things that I enjoy, that are part of me, that give me comfort and that give my life meaning. . . . I would miss going to Mass, I would miss the feeling of joy that I feel during the holidays, that Jesus was born on Christmas and then at Easter when He rises from the dead and returns to life. I would miss the songs and the interactions of people at church. I would miss part of an identity of myself as my family, and how I identify myself. It's not the first thing about me. I don't say, "Hi, I'm Sarah, I'm Catholic." But it is a part of who I am, and I feel like being raised in the Catholic Church sort of helped me be what I am. . . . I want to be a psychologist. Being raised in the Catholic Church taught me how to try to make the world a better place by helping others. I think if you're going to go to church and be Catholic and do more than just kind of go through the motions, you would have to kind of have that sense of obligation in this world.

Interviewer: You said earlier that you have a fiancé who is also Catholic. What
   if you have children?
Sarah: My fiancé and I have discussed that when we do have children, we
   would raise them Catholic. He was also raised Catholic. We both agreed that
   it's very important to raise our children in the Church. Whether it's the
   Catholic Church, Presbyterian Church, or whatever may not be as important. But because we're Catholic, we know all the Catholic stuff. There's
   nothing that I disagree with in the Catholic Church that I can't talk to my
   kids about on some level. I don't think I would raise them terribly strictly,
   like you *must* do all of these things. But I want them to learn about the sacraments, I want them to learn about Jesus, I want them to attend church and
   go to CCD. and learn about the Ten Commandments and about the Bible.
   And I also want to have that family community. I want holidays to have
   more of a meaning than just commercial meaning, because that was a big
   part of my childhood.

Sarah exemplifies the wide tolerance zone we discovered in our research.
This raises the question, Are Catholics like Sarah, who are tolerant of other
religions' truth claims, different from other Catholics? For example, do they
remain Catholic? Yes, research shows that not many leave the Church. Do
they attend Church and participate in parish life? Yes, they do, but at lower
rates than other Catholics. For example, on the 2003 survey statement "the
Catholic religion has no more spiritual truth than other major religions,"
the persons agreeing attend Mass weekly less frequently than those dis-
agreeing (17 percentage points lower), and they are less often registered in
local parishes (10 percentage points lower). Persons agreeing with the statement "If you believe in God, it doesn't really matter which religion you
belong to" attend Mass less often (25 percentage points less attend weekly)
and less frequently register in parishes (10 percentage points lower). These
responses—which could also be seen as indications of religious relativ-
ism—are associated with lower levels of Church commitment. They do not
prevent regular Mass attendance and commitment to parish life, but they
seem to weaken it.

In short, American Catholics are quite committed to their faith and their
Church, but they do not believe that Catholicism has the truth and that
other religions do not. Their commitment no longer includes claims of
being the one true Church.

CONCLUSION

All observers are saying that Catholic identity has been shifting. Our findings and the findings of other researchers describe this shift with more pre-
cision. We have found that most Catholics attach quite a high importance

to their identity as Catholics, although young people do so less than their elders. The core of Catholicism in the minds of laypeople is in the realm of creedal beliefs, sacraments, devotion to Mary the Mother of God, and service to the poor. Other elements of Catholicism are seen as peripheral and therefore changeable, including specific moral teachings and specific institutional rules related to issues such as the priesthood. Young Catholics see these specific moral teachings—especially regarding sexuality and marriage—as peripheral to the faith, and well-educated young Catholics see them as even more so.

What does it take to be a good Catholic? In lay opinion, it requires creedal belief and receiving sacraments, not specific behavior such as weekly Church attendance or obeying teachings about birth control. We also found that, even as they embrace the core teachings of their own faith, Catholics are quite tolerant about the truth claims of other religions. They tend to believe that all religions have at least some truth. Thus, interfaith boundaries are not as clear today as they were, say, fifty to one hundred years ago.

In the next chapter, we turn to Catholics' commitment to the institutional Church.

3

American Catholics' Commitment to the Institutional Church

A central concern of our four surveys has been to track the changing nature and level of commitment that American Catholics have to the Church as a formal institution and to the articles of faith proclaimed by the Church. This chapter looks at commitment to the Church as an institution. It has two purposes: 1) to see which portions of the Catholic laity are highly committed or less committed to the Church and 2) to depict clearly the most committed Catholics. It is often argued that the most committed Catholics are the people researchers should look at most closely because they are the foundation of parish life. We describe them here.

The first question before us is how to measure commitment to the Church. By "commitment" we mean the degree to which a person entrusts a significant part of his or her beliefs, values, and behavior to the institutional Roman Catholic Church. Research scholars and pollsters have traditionally used attendance at religious services as the best single predictor of church members' commitment to their denominations' religious beliefs and practices. In the 2004 election, the scholars consistently found that attendance at church services was related to key issues such as abortion and same-sex marriage (Langer and Cohen 2005; Pew Research Center 2005). Americans who attended religious services at least once a week were more likely to be conservative and to support the political party whose position was closer to their beliefs on these issues.

In this chapter we look at Church commitment more broadly. A distinction between the Catholic faith and commitment to the institutional Church is understandable to some Catholics but not to others. Many Catholics do make the distinction, and when they do, it is often to clarify where their strongest commitments lie. In addition, some Catholics point out the difference, when talking about their own Church commitments, between local parish life and the hierarchy of the Church. Distinctions such as these are important to know about, insofar as people make them.

Here we look at how different levels of commitment to the Church relate to the laity's specific beliefs and practices. As we will see, the linkages are not always strong. Just as the laity's subjective perception of their personal identities may differ from the Catholic Church's official teachings about Catholic identity, so also even high commitment to the Church as institution does not preclude holding beliefs and attitudes that are at odds with Catholic teachings. Today some American Catholics insist that unless one is totally committed to all the teachings currently held by the Vatican, one cannot be considered a good Catholic. Others respect the great body of Church teachings but argue that reason and faith combine to create a Catholic conscience that allows for disagreement on noninfallible teachings. For example, Elissa Lieberg, a college student, responded to a *Commonweal* article on a Catholic doctor's dilemma with young women patients who seek a prescription for the birth control pill:

> Throughout my years in parochial school and religious education classes, the teachings of the Catholic Church were emphasized and not to be questioned. The Church's views were especially stressed in the areas of the use of birth control and sex. Recently, however, as a student at the College of St. Benedict, I have learned about the primacy of conscience, and how this is an important aspect of the Catholic faith. In "A Doctor's Dilemma" (September 23) Lynn Beth Satterly stresses this idea, and she focuses on how she uses her own judgment and not the judgment of the Church in her job as a family practice doctor. Her points are extremely important; the basic idea of the primacy of conscience needs to be stressed more often in the teachings of the faith. (Lieberg 2005, 26)

The linkages between these very different visions of the good Catholic and levels of Church commitment are strong but not perfect. In addition, our longitudinal research enables us to note the areas of stability and change in these beliefs, practices, and attitudes. As our story unfolds, we will see that Catholics have various levels of commitment to their faith and to their Church, and they seem comfortable with making distinctions. Having high commitment to the Church does not mean that the person has blind obedience to its teachings.

In our book *Laity American and Catholic: Transforming the Church* (D'Antonio et al. 1996), we began trying to find a better predictor of Catholic beliefs, practices, and attitudes than Mass attendance alone. Clearly, regular Mass attenders were more orthodox than the others in their commitment to official Church teachings. But when asked about how important the Church was to them personally, less than two-thirds (61 percent) said it was the most important or among the most important parts of their lives. And when we asked if they would ever leave the Church, we found a range of responses. To encompass these dimensions, we constructed a Church Commitment Index based on the responses to the questions regarding the frequency of Mass attendance, importance of the Catholic Church in their lives, and whether they would ever consider leaving the Catholic Church.[1]

Table 3.1 shows changes in the three indicators over time. All of them declined, but the decline in Mass attendance was the most significant. It is the measure most responsible for the decline in the percentage of highly committed Catholics from 27 percent in 1987 to 21 percent in 2005. Overall, there was more stability than change among Catholics during this eighteen-year period.

LEVELS OF COMMITMENT:
A DEMOGRAPHIC PORTRAIT

Table 3.2 provides important information about levels of Church commitment in the American Catholic population. The most noteworthy finding is that pre–Vatican II Catholics, who now constitute only 17 percent of the adult Catholic population, are the most highly committed to the Church. In 1987, when they constituted one-third of all Catholics, 44 percent were highly committed; that figure has remained stable over time (it was 43 percent in 2005). Thus, one reason for the gradual decline in the percentage of high commitment Catholics from 1987 to 2005 is the diminished number of pre–Vatican II Catholics.

Twenty percent of Vatican II Catholics had high commitment scores in 2005, a decline of 7 percentage points from the 1999 survey. Among post–Vatican II Catholics, who now constitute 40 percent of the adult Catholic population, 17 percent scored high in commitment, the same as in 1987. The Millennials (9 percent of the total) included nobody who scored high. Whether this is simply an expression of youthful desire to be free of religious bonds that may change later remains to be seen.

Because older Catholics have higher commitment than young adults, one cannot expect any increase in high-commitment Catholics in the near future. The younger Catholics attend Mass less often. As the number of pre–Vatican II Catholics continues its decline, so also will the overall rate of Mass attendance.

As table 3.2 shows, women are more likely than men to be high in commitment, but from other research, we know that the difference has dimin-

---

1. For a description of the three variables used to construct the Index of Commitment, see chapter 1.

Table 3.1.   Indicators of Commitment to the Church, 1987–2005 (in percentages)

	1987	*1993*	*1999*	*2005*
	%	%	%	%
How important is the Catholic Church to you personally?				
("the most important or among the most important parts of your life")	49	43	44	44
On a scale of 1 to 7, with 1 being "I would never leave the Catholic Church and 7 being "Yes, I might leave the Catholic Church," where would you place yourself on this scale?				
(percentage placing 1 or 2)	64	61	57	56
How often do you attend Mass?				
(at least once a week)	44	43	37	34
Commitment Index Score				
High	27	23	23	21
Medium	57	59	60	64
Low	16	18	17	15

ished over time (D'Antonio et al. 2001). Married Catholics—and especially those married in the Church—are more likely than nonmarried and those married outside the Church to be high in commitment. Hispanic Catholics, who are rapidly becoming the largest ethnic group of Catholics, are below average in commitment, although Catholics at both the lowest and the highest income levels scored above the average in level of commitment. The biggest difference was found between registered parishioners (29 percent highly committed) and Catholics who were not registered in any parish (only 9 percent highly committed).

The highly committed Catholics provide the core elements of parish life. They provide the leadership, volunteer labor, and crucial financial support. They are the lectors and Eucharistic ministers who have become vital parts of contemporary parish life. They are also among the more than 33,000 lay Catholics who work within the institutional Church at parish and diocesan levels. A large portion of the most committed are old and thus not likely to be around to serve the Church in coming decades. Vatican II Catholics, now moving into their senior earning years and with more time available as responsibility for children's education ends, will become the core of parish life. Their Church commitment is strong. The post–Vatican II generation is similar. Because the Millennial generation is small in our sample, we must be cautious about its responses.

Table 3.2.   Level of Commitment in Demographic Categories, 2005 (in percentages added horizontally)

	Commitment		
	High %	Medium %	Low %
All Catholics	21	64	15
Generation			
Pre–Vatican II (born 1940 or earlier)	43	46	12
Vatican II (born 1941–1960)	20	68	12
Post–Vatican II (born 1961–1978)	17	67	16
Millennials (1979–1987)	0	73	27
Gender			
Female	23	64	13
Male	19	64	17
Marital status			
Married	24	64	12
Other	15	64	17
Marriage approved by Church			
Yes	30	61	9
No	9	68	23
Education			
High school or less	24	65	11
Some college	19	66	15
College graduate or more	21	61	18
Hispanic origin			
Yes	15	69	16
No	22	63	14
Income			
Under $50,000	23	62	16
$50,000–$75,000	16	70	14
$75,000–$100,000	19	66	15
Over $100,000	27	58	15
Registered member of parish			
Yes	29	64	7
No	9	31	60

COMMITMENT AND IDENTITY

We expected that laity with a strong sense of Catholic identity would also score high on their commitment to the Church, and that was the case. Table 3.3 shows the relationship between Catholic identity and Church commitment. Almost half of the Catholics who scored high on the Identity Index also scored high on the Church Commitment Index.

Table 3.4 provides further information about the relationship between commitment and Catholics' views of their faith and their Church. As

Table 3.3. Relation between Catholic Identity and Level of Commitment, 2005 (in percentages)

		Identity Index		
		Low %	Medium %	High %
Church Commitment Index				
Low		44	3	1
Medium		55	76	51
High		1	21	47
	Total	100	100	99

expected, the vast majority of high-commitment Catholics say that being Catholic is important, that the sacraments are essential, that they want young people in their families to be Catholic, that they cannot imagine being anything but Catholic, and that the Catholic Church has a larger share of the truth than other religions do. However, eight in ten also believe that how a person lives is more important than being Catholic.

This is not surprising. In a pluralistic society like ours, with acknowledged non-Catholic heroes like Martin Luther King Jr., Rosa Parks, and Abraham Lincoln, Catholics may well hold that their religion contains more truth than others while at the same time being able to appreciate the lives well lived by so many people of different faiths.

A majority of medium-commitment Catholics also agreed with the items on the importance of faith and the Church. At the same time, nine in ten say being Catholic is not as important as how one lives one's life, and barely half believe that Catholicism has a greater share of truth.

Low-commitment Catholics agree with the statement that the sacraments

Table 3.4. Catholics Who Agree with Certain Beliefs and Attitudes, by Commitment, 2005 (in percentages)

	Commitment Level		
	High %	Medium %	Low %
Percentages who strongly or somewhat agree:			
Being Catholic is important part of who you are	100	91	43
Sacraments an essential part of relationship with God	99	82	53
Important that younger generation of family be Catholic	96	83	34
I cannot imagine being anything other than Catholic	94	71	28
How a person lives more important than being Catholic	84	91	85
Catholicism has a greater share of truth than other religions	82	56	19

are an essential park of their relationship with God. They too agree that one's lifestyle (being a good person) is more important than one's religious affiliation (just being Catholic). But they scored lower than other Catholics on all of the other items on faith in the Church. Being Catholic is not an important part of who they are, nor is it important that the younger generation of their families be Catholics, and only one in five agrees at all that Catholicism has a greater share of truth than other religions.

We expected commitment to affect how Catholics view the teachings of the Church on matters of faith and morals. The higher one's commitment, the more reasons one would have to embrace the Church's teachings. The lower one's commitment, the fewer reasons one would have to accept the Church's teachings and the more reasons to question them. How strong are the relationships? Table 3.5 displays our findings on what Catholics believe it takes to be a good Catholic and relates aspects of identity to commitment.

People who identify themselves as Catholics but have a low level of commitment to the Church see significantly fewer requirements for being a good Catholic than those who are highly committed. The latter perceive more requirements of belief and actions than do the low- and medium-commitment Catholics. Even in regard to the two most central creedal beliefs (the first two items in table 3.5) having to do with Jesus' life, death, resurrection, and presence in the Eucharist, they differ by more than 30 percentage points. Only on the question of donating time or money to help the poor is there any semblance of agreement among the three categories of Catholics.

Comparison of medium-level Catholics with the highly committed produces mixed results. Strong majorities of both categories agree that one cannot be a good Catholic without believing in the Real Presence of Jesus in

Table 3.5. What It Takes to Be Considered a Good Catholic, by Level of Commitment, 2005 (percentages agreeing)

	High %	Medium %	Low %
Percentage agreeing that you can be a good Catholic without . . .			
Believing in Jesus' resurrection	11	21	46
Believing in the real presence of Jesus	21	37	54
Donating time or money to help the poor	30	48	48
Obeying the Church's teaching on abortion	31	63	76
Donating time or money to help the parish	40	60	80
Divorce and remarriage without the Church	43	69	84
Marriage approved by the Church	49	70	84
Going to church every Sunday	49	81	95
Obeying the Church's teaching on birth control	64	76	89

the Eucharist and in the life, death, and resurrection of Jesus. Beyond that, the only other area of agreement is on birth control, in which strong majorities of all three categories agree that obedience to this teaching is not essential to being a good Catholic. Regarding the teachings on regular weekly Mass attendance, having one's marriage approved by the Church, remarriage without a Church annulment, and obeying the teaching on abortion, a majority of medium-committed Catholics did not see dissent from these teachings as preventing them from being good Catholics. On the other hand, a majority of all three categories of Catholics agreed that one cannot be a good Catholic without donating time or money to help the poor. Aid to the poor has roots in Jewish scriptures and is one of the subjects on which Jesus preached at length. It is formulated in considerable detail in the Catechism and finds its way into many pieces of legislation at the federal and local levels.[2]

IMPORTANCE OF CHURCH TEACHINGS

Table 3.6 redirects the focus from requirement for being a good Catholic to the beliefs, teachings, and practices respondents said were very important to them. High-, medium-, and low-commitment Catholics are quite different in this connection.

Table 3.6. Agreement on Which Aspects of the Catholic Religion Are Very Important to Them as Catholics, by Commitment Level, 2005 (in percentages)

	Commitment Level		
	High %	*Medium* %	*Low* %
Aspects of the Catholic religion that are very important:			
The sacraments	100	77	37
Jesus' resurrection	95	88	52
Helping the poor	93	84	73
Mary as Mother of God	94	76	35
Devotions such as the rosary	79	49	10
Church teaching on abortion	76	39	18
Regular daily prayer life	75	51	34
Church teaching on same-sex marriage	72	45	21
Teaching authority claimed by the Vatican	71	38	16
Church teachings on social justice	62	47	27
A celibate male clergy	44	29	11

2. See DiIulio (2006). DiIulio points out how difficult it is to translate one's commitment to help the needy into concrete legislation.

High-commitment Catholics are almost unanimous in declaring that the sacraments, Jesus' resurrection, helping the poor, and belief in Mary as the Mother of God were very important to them personally. Three out of four medium-committed Catholics also declared that these four beliefs were very important to them. Among the low-committed Catholics, only Jesus' resurrection and helping the poor were deemed very important by a majority. The only item that a majority of high-commitment Catholics did not see as very important to them personally was the Vatican teaching requiring a celibate male clergy. Otherwise, seven out of ten of the high-commitment Catholics said the teaching authority of the Vatican was very important to them, as was borne out by the importance they gave to teachings on abortion and same-sex marriage.

PUBLIC POLICY AND COMMITMENT

Our final topic is the influence of Church commitment on attitudes about public policy issues. We first probed this area in 1999 and so are able to compare 1999 and 2005 findings. We asked about five policy issues, the first two of which the U.S. bishops support and the last three of which they oppose. In constructing our five-part question, we did not explicitly state the bishops' interest in these issues. We began our question with "Following are some questions about social and political issues. Please tell me whether you agree or disagree with each of these issues." Table 3.7 presents the relationship between level of commitment and responses to these five issues. The first advocated more government funds for health care for poor children. Most polls have shown that a majority of Americans support this, but only the high-commitment Catholics were steadfast in their support over

Table 3.7.　Catholics Who Agree with Certain Beliefs and Attitudes, by Commitment, 2005 (in percentages)

	Commitment Level					
	High		*Medium*		*Low*	
	1999 %	*2005* %	*1999* %	*2005* %	*1999* %	*2005* %
Percentages strongly agreeing:						
More government funds for health care	71	71	74	67	74	63
Reduced spending on nuclear arms	48	35	51	38	57	41
More funds for military	39	43	35	39	24	32
Stiffer enforcement of the death penalty	48	24	56	33	61	40
More cutbacks in welfare programs	19	16	27	16	24	23

time. Medium- and low-commitment Catholics weakened slightly in their support. Still, the majority of all the respondents were in support.

Second, reducing spending on nuclear arms has been a policy position of the bishops that has its roots in the Peace Pastoral of 1983. In 1999, a majority of all Catholics strongly supported reducing spending on nuclear arms. However, the events of 9/11 seem to have had an impact on the laity; in 2005, less than 40 percent strongly supported reducing spending on nuclear arms, and seemingly the level of commitment did not affect layperson's attitudes. The public has been subjected to periodic warnings about the dangers of a nuclear war posed by Iraq, Iran, and North Korea, which may well have caused the decline in the percentages wanting less funding for nuclear weaponry.

Third, this same change in perception of the world of 2005 versus the world of 1999 is found in the slight increase in Catholic support for more funds for the military—a policy not favored by the U.S. bishops. Catholics continue to make a distinction between support for nuclear weapons and government funds for the military.

Fourth, from 1999 to 2005, Catholics of all commitment levels became much less likely to support stiffer enforcement of the death penalty. The level of support for the death penalty in 2005 was only one in four among the high-commitment Catholics and one in three among the medium-commitment group. Although this question does not address abolishment of or a moratorium on the death penalty, it does show that a majority of Catholics oppose stricter enforcement. For their part, the bishops have followed the lead of the late John Paul II and mounted an increasingly consistent policy against the death penalty, even as Catholic writers (such as Peggy Noonan) and Supreme Court Justices (such as Antonin Scalia) insist that this is not an infallible teaching, so it can be an issue in which conscience takes precedence. Despite that kind of resistance from conservative Catholics, it is an issue in which the bishops appear to be gaining voice. The movement against the death penalty has also been aided by the determined efforts of Sister Helen Prejean, with her appearances on television, her lectures, and her book *Dead Man Walking*.

Fifth, the welfare reform legislation of 1996 failed to remove welfare programs from the public agenda. In fact, the number of Americans living in poverty and in need of some form of assistance has increased again since 2000. In 1999, only one in four Catholics strongly agreed that there should be more "cutbacks in welfare programs." Six years later, in 2005, only one in five strongly agreed with further cuts. The trends, although small, are in the direction advocated by the bishops.

A review of the findings on these five issues that have been part of the public and bishops' agenda in recent years shows mixed results regarding the influence of Church commitment. Only on the issue of the death penalty did high-commitment Catholics significantly differ from the others. At the other end, low-commitment Catholics were the least supportive of more funds for the military. Overall, the findings indicate that American Catholics and their bishops are on the same page in regard to at least four of the five issues; the death penalty issue is not as clear-cut. Whether this results from an awareness and acceptance of the bishops' teachings on these issues is indeterminate.

CONCLUSION

Our analysis of the relationship between laypersons' commitment to the Catholic Church and its teachings reveals variation within and across commitment lines. Overall, the level of Church commitment has moved gradually downward. The percentage of high-commitment American Catholics declined from 27 percent in 1987 to 21 percent in 2005. At the low end there has been no increase; the percentage scoring low in church commitment has been constant at about 15 percent.[3] Thus, about two out of three Catholics are in the middle category. Considering the dramatic twists and turns in the Catholic Church at home and abroad during the papacy of John Paul II, the sex abuse scandal, and the conflict over the question of homosexuality, this stability in level of Church commitment is noteworthy.

The area of greatest instability lies with the declining percentage of the Church's most highly committed Catholics. Since 1987, more than four in ten of pre–Vatican II Catholics, now 65 years of age or older, have remained highly committed to the Church. The drop in overall commitment level is mostly a function of the declining numbers of older Catholics and growing numbers of the young.

High commitment by a Catholic does not automatically yield complete compliance with the teachings of the Vatican or the U.S. Catholic Bishops. For example, the Vatican continues to state that contraceptive birth control, like abortion, is an intrinsic evil. Yet 64 percent of the most highly committed said you could be a good Catholic while not obeying the Church's teaching on birth control, and even on abortion 31 percent said this. And since 1987, four in ten of the high-commitment Catholics have supported the idea of ordaining women to the priesthood. Extrapolating from these figures, it is probable that Catholics who claim to support all the Church's

---

3. See Greeley (1989, 194, 195, 198). Greeley made the point that given all the turbulence and scandal of the 1970s and 1980s, it was encouraging that such a small percentage of Catholics might leave (he used only point 7 on the 1-to-7 scale as an indicator of "might leave." In our 2005 survey, only 8 percent of American Catholics checked point 7, adding strength to Greeley's thesis and to ours.

teachings on all matters may constitute no more than one-third of the highly committed, or 7 percent of all Catholics. Numerous high-commitment Catholics find space to support the ordination of women, the use of contraceptive birth control, lay involvement in the selection of priests for their parish, and women as deacons. They may simply be taking seriously Vatican II teachings on freedom of conscience informed by reason and faith.

4

The Sacraments: Trends and Variations

The Catholic Church teaches that "Christ now acts through the sacraments he instituted to communicate his grace" (*Catechism* 1084). The seven Catholic sacraments include three sacraments of initiation (Baptism, Eucharist, and Confirmation), two sacraments of vocation (Marriage and Holy Orders), and two sacraments of healing (Reconciliation and Anointing of the Sick).

These sacraments were a topic of conversation one rainy morning when the mother and daughter we introduced you to in chapter 1 met at their favorite coffee shop. The subject came up when the mother casually mentioned that she had gone to Confession the day before. "I felt like I needed to talk about a couple of things, so I went," she told her daughter. "As it turned out, my favorite priest, Father John, was there. He listened carefully to everything I had to say, then asked me a couple of good questions. After we talked a bit, he thanked me for coming in, urged me to pray about my concerns, and told me to leave the rest up to God."

The daughter looked at her Mom for a second, then asked, "What do you need to go to Confession for? God knows, if there's anybody who follows the Ten Commandments and the rules of the Church, it's you!"

"Honey," the mother replied, "the sacraments are God's way of reaching out to us. They are his way of being part of our daily lives. We should participate in them as often as we possibly can, including Confession."

"I agree that the sacraments are one way that we can be in touch with God, but they're not the only way," the daughter responded. "If I have something on my mind, and I want to talk it over with God, I go to him directly. My favorite times to do that are when I take my morning walk in the neighborhood and when I sit on the front porch after dinner. I don't need to go through a priest I don't know at a parish I don't belong to. Besides, you know I don't like all the Church's rules about who can and who cannot participate in the other sacraments. As long as I believe in the core teachings of the Church—you know, that God became human, died for our sins, and rose from the dead—then I don't need to go to Mass every week, just because the Church says so. If my boyfriend weren't Catholic, I don't think God would mind if we got married by a justice of the peace. And, if I'm honest with myself about women's rights, I don't think the priesthood should be limited to men. Women should be priests too."

The mother sighed, then said, "I love you, baby, but we sure think differently about some things. How about a refill on the coffee, and then let's talk about something else."

How many Catholics think as the mother does in this conversation? How many think as the daughter does? How important are the sacraments to today's Catholics? How many Catholics adhere to traditional Church teachings about the sacraments, and how many think teachings related to these sacraments should be revised (for example, to ordain women)? Are Catholics as likely to participate in the Eucharist and marry in the Church as they did, let us say, fifty to one hundred years ago?

Whatever the central tendencies and overarching trends might be, there also are likely to be variations among Catholics on these issues. Hence, we also ask, Which Catholics are like the mother and believe that they have a duty to participate in the sacraments, and which ones are like the daughter and feel no such obligation? Which ones think Church rules about access to the sacraments ought to remain as they are, and which ones want to modify them? Which Catholics are most actively involved in the sacraments, and which ones seldom, if ever, participate in them?

PREVIOUS ATTEMPTS TO SEEK ANSWERS TO THESE QUESTIONS

We are not the first people to ask these questions. For more than a century, the Church has asked dioceses to keep track of how many Catholics participate in several of the sacraments and has published the data in the *Official Catholic Directory* (OCD). For many decades, Church leaders and researchers have used these data to chart trends in the number of baptisms, confirmations, and marriages that are performed in the Church each year. The *OCD* also has provided data on the total number of priests, although it has not reported the number of ordinations until very recently. Starting in the 1980s, it has also published data on the number of confirmations performed annually.

Unfortunately, the *OCD* does not contain any information on the number of Catholics participating in the sacrament of Reconciliation. Nor does it report the number of people experiencing the Anointing of the Sick. It also does not indicate how many Catholics are getting married "outside of the Church" (that is, are entering into marriages that are not recorded or approved by the Church). Nor does it report Catholics' beliefs about the importance of the sacraments or their attitudes about the rules and regulations governing their implementation. We have to turn to historians and social researchers for information on these issues.

Historians such as Dolan (1985, 2002), McGreevy (1996), and Morris (1997) have done their best to estimate the frequency of Catholics' participation in the sacraments in the past. Using parish records, newspaper accounts, and personal diaries, these scholars have documented fluctuations in sacramental participation over time. Social researchers began asking questions about the sacraments in the 1950s. Father Joseph Fichter led the way, reporting high levels of participation but also showing—much to the dismay of some Church leaders—that a sizable number of Catholics were not in compliance with Church standards. His famous distinction between "nuclear," "modal," "marginal," and "dormant" Catholics reflected the variations he found among laypeople (Fichter 1954, 21–30). Other researchers, such as Gerhard Lenski (1961), reported similar findings, noting extraordinarily high levels of "doctrinal orthodoxy" and "associational" involvement (including participation in the Eucharist) but also recording important variations. By the 1960s and 1970s, Father Andrew Greeley also was charting Catholics' views of and participation in the sacraments. Even as he documented some decline in rates of sacramental participation, he emphasized the persistence of a "sacramental imagination" and its impact on Catholics' religious practices (Greeley 1977, 1990, 2000). Starting in the 1980s, we also have monitored Catholics' involvement in the sacraments (D'Antonio et al. 1989, 1996, 2001; Davidson et al. 1997). In our 1999 study, we documented declining levels of religious practice and compliance with Church teachings.

In this chapter, we use these data to document trends in sacramental participation and offer an interpretation of changes that have taken place in the past century. Our examination of trends includes all sacraments, but our analysis of Catholics' current attitudes and actions omits Holy Orders, which we discuss in more detail in chapter 5. We also describe variations in Catholics' current religious beliefs and practices relating to the sacraments. Finally, Catholic identity and commitment to the Church are at the core of our effort to explain which Catholics have traditional views of the sacraments and which have progressive views.

TRENDS

After reviewing the historical record, some observers, including Dolan (2002) and Greeley (1999,2004), have concluded that the Church is stronger now than it was in the 1950s and that it is moving in the right direction. Others, such as Varacalli (2000) and Carlin (2003), say the 1950s and early 1960s were the golden era of the Church and that the Church has been in a free fall ever since. Others, notably Steinfels (2003) and Gibson (2003), believe that the Church is adrift and struggling to find its way.

We offer a different interpretation. Ours begins with the assumption that sacramental participation rates reflect the prevailing social and religious conditions at any point in time. As these conditions change, we should expect Catholics' views of and participation in the sacraments to change. In addition, rather than starting with the 1950s, we take a longer view, going back to the early 1900s. We will show that the social and religious conditions in the early 1900s produced rather modest levels of sacramental participation. As those conditions changed, Catholics adapted by becoming more involved in all phases of Church life, including the sacraments, during the 1940s and 1950s. As conditions have changed again, Catholics have adapted. This time the adaptation involves less dependency on the Church and less participation in the sacraments. Accordingly, rather than seeing the 1950s as the standard by which we should judge all previous and future periods, we see it as just one of many periods in Catholic history, albeit one that produced unusually high levels of participation.

The Early 1900s

The early 1900s was a time of large-scale immigration, with Irish, Italian, German, and Polish Catholics coming to the United States and trying to establish a new life. In 1900, there were only about 12 million Catholics in the United States (about 16 percent of the total population). That number grew to about 16 million in 1910 and about 20 million in 1920 (at which point Catholics were up to 19 percent of the U.S. population). Half of all U.S. Catholics lived in the Northeast (Morris 1997, 113). Although the Church had a strong presence in urban areas, "it was weak in the country areas, in the South and West and in rural districts" (Bausch 1989, 507).

The laity's attention was focused on finding work, meeting their families' immediate needs, and sacrificing for their children, whom they hoped would enjoy a better standard of living. They asked God for help but knew that being Catholic—or being known as a Catholic—meant one had to deal with religious prejudice and discrimination (Dolan 2002; Higham 1988; Perlmutter 1999). As a result, some Catholics distanced themselves from the Church, changing their names and converting to Protestantism. Others turned to the Church at significant points in their lives (such as weddings and funerals), but the Church was not the center of their lives. Many worked on Sundays, and the Church—which did not yet have the organizational base it developed later—was of only limited assistance in meeting the laity's immediate needs.

These conditions yielded uneven levels of participation in the sacraments (Dolan 2002; Gillis 1999; McGreevy 1996; Morris 1997). Although rigorous statistical data are hard to come by, most historical studies show that Baptism, Confirmation, Marriage, and Last Rites were important, once-in-a-lifetime markers for Catholics. The vast majority of Catholics baptized their children and had them confirmed in the Church. They also wanted their sons and daughters to marry other Catholics and to marry in the Church, which most of them did (Dolan 1985, 228). When family members were nearing the end of their lives, Catholics called a priest and asked for Last Rites.

Participation in other sacraments was spottier. Parents made sure their children received their first Communion and went to Holy Communion as long as they lived at home. After that, they were pretty much on their own. At key points in the year—especially Christmas and Easter—laypeople would flock to Confession and Communion, but participation was much lower the rest of the year. People did not look forward to Confession. Moreover, the Church's emphasis on holiness of the clergy but the sinfulness of the laity fostered a widespread belief that laypeople were not worthy enough to receive the Eucharist on a regular basis. The Church also did not emphasize the need to receive Holy Communion on a regular basis until Pope Pius X got behind the "Communion movement" in 1905. Although Mass attendance and reception of the Eucharist increased during this period, "devotional Catholicism"—emphasizing "Mass and sacraments"— did not reach its "high-water mark" until "the 1920–1950 era" (Dolan 2002, 169).

Of all the ethnic groups, the Irish produced the largest number of priests, but, overall, priestly vocations barely kept up with the rapidly expanding Catholic population. By 1900, there were about 12 million Catholics and about 12,000 priests (thus, a ratio of only one priest for every 1,000 laypeople [D'Antonio et al 2001, 12]). The situation improved only slightly during the next two decades. By 1920, there were 20 million laypeople and 21,000 priests (a ratio of one priest for every 951 laypeople).

Mid-Century

By the 1950s, these European immigrants were still working class, but they were gaining a foothold in American society. With their help, the

Church built an immense network of Catholic institutions known as the "Catholic ghetto" (Cogley and Van Allen 1986). This highly segregated enclave protected Catholics from religious prejudice and discrimination (Massa 2001). It also provided the means by which the Church passed the faith from one generation to the next. That faith included an image of God as a stern judge and a view of the laity as people who were prone to sin. As a result, laypeople believed that the road to heaven was narrow and that the road to hell was wide. They turned to the Church for help, both socially and spiritually.

These conditions gave rise to very high levels of sacramental participation (see table 4.1). Wanting to make sure their children would go to heaven (and not limbo), Catholic "parents routinely presented their child for baptism within the first few weeks of life" (Gillis 1999, 159). Thus, as the Catholic population grew, reaching 24 million in 1945 and 46 million in 1965, baptisms also increased to 793,000 in 1945 and 1.4 million in 1965. Ratios of one baptism for every thirty-one Catholics in 1945 and one for every thirty-three Catholics in 1965 indicated that baptisms were keeping up with the growing Catholic population.

The emphasis on early childhood socialization also was reflected in parents' emphasis on making sure their children made their first Confession and received their first Communion at an early age (usually by the time they were seven to nine years old). Nuns taught young Catholics about the importance of these sacraments and took young Catholics through practice sessions, showing them exactly what to expect when they would actually go to Confession and Communion for the first time. Meanwhile, parents made, rented, or bought special clothes, and family members prepared for this special occasion. Confessions were usually held on Saturday and first Communions on the following day. Although precise statistics are nearly impossible to find, it is estimated that about 70 percent of baptized infants went on to first Communion (Fichter 1951, 62, 94–95). Family albums and historical accounts are filled with pictures showing little boys in white suits and little girls in white dresses and veils, with their hands in praying position, having their pictures taken in front of the church.

There are no national statistics on the number of Confirmations during this period. However, Fichter (1951, 94–95) reports that, in the New Orleans parish he studied, 98 percent of all eligible parishioners (twelve or more years of age) had been confirmed. He also estimated that about half the infants baptized between 1932 and 1936 (and who, therefore, would be eligible for Confirmation in the mid-1940s) were actually confirmed between 1944 and 1948. Catholics who lived through this period recall large numbers of teenagers learning about the saints, selecting saints they liked, and picking a saint's name as their own. All this was in preparation for Confirmation, including a special Mass at which the area bishop pre-

Table 4.1. Participation in the Sacraments, 1945–2004

	1945	1965	1985	1995	2005
Total Catholics	24,402,124	46,246,175	52,654,908	56,980,797	63,952,550
Sacraments of initiation					
Baptisms	792,987	1,398,087	1,041,319	1,119,700	1,006,150
Ratio of baptisms to total Catholics	1:31	1:33	1:51	1:51	1:64
Eucharist (% attending Mass weekly/ % receiving Communion weekly)	75/40	70/?	53/39	43/36	34/?
Confirmations	—	—	—	576,887	610,282
Ratio of confirmations to total Catholics	—	—	—	1:99	1:104
Sacraments of vocation					
Marriages	245,261	355,182	348,300	292,499	207:112
Ratios of marriages to total Catholics	1:99	1:130	1:151	1:195	1:323
Ordinations	814	1,118	711	583	431
Ratio of ordinations to total Catholics	1:29,978	1:41,365	1:74,057	1:97,737	1:148,382

Note: The Church does not record data on the total number of people going to Confession or receiving Anointing of the Sick, so the table does not include any data on these sacraments of healing. See text for a discussion of data from other sources. Sources: For 1945, Davidson (2005, 162); for 1965 and 1985, Gallup and Castelli (1987, 194–95); Morris (1997, 308); for 1995, Davidson (2005, 151); for 2005, OCD. Ordination statistics for 1945–1995 are from *Annuario Pontificio*; for 2004, they are from *OCD*. Total priests and ratio of priests to total Catholics are as follows: 1945 (38,980; 1:626), 1965 (59,193; 1:781), 1985 (57,183; 1:921), 1995 (47,511; 1:1,199), and 2005 (41,472; 1:542).

sided. Young people being confirmed often shuddered at the prospect of having to come before the bishop, say something about the saint they had chosen, and receive a slap that symbolized their need to be strong and stand up for their faith.

The *OCD* does not provide data on the sacrament of Reconciliation, but historical accounts and surveys report high levels of participation in the mid-1900s. Fichter (1951, 55), for example, reported that 79 percent of parishioners went to Confession at least once a year in the 1950s. Greeley (1977, 127) reported that 82 percent of Catholics did so in 1963.

The rate of Mass attendance rose to the point that about 70 to 75 percent of Catholics attended Mass every week in the middle of the twentieth century. However, it is estimated that only 40 to 60 percent of the people attending Mass felt worthy enough to receive Holy Communion. When it came time for Communion, many people remained in their seats.

As the size of the Catholic population grew, so did the number of Catholic marriages. There were about 245,000 in 1945 and nearly 355,000 in 1965. But the ratios of one marriage for every 94 Catholics in 1945 and one for every 130 Catholics in 1965 indicate that the number of marriages approved by the Church was not keeping pace with the expanding population base. This slowdown reflected the fact that an increasing number of Catholics were entering into interfaith marriages and that more and more marriages were taking place "outside the Church" (that is, without being recognized by the Church).

Priestly vocations increased dramatically between the early 1900s and the middle of the century: 814 new priests were ordained in 1945; 1,118 in 1965. The total number of priests climbed from 21,000 in 1920 to nearly 44,000 in 1950 and 59,000 in 1965. There seemed to be an abundance of priests. However, the increases in ordinations and priests actually were not keeping up with the increase in the total Catholic population. In 1945, there was one ordination for every 29,978 laypeople and one priest for every 626 Catholics. By 1965, there was only one ordination for every 41,365 Catholics and only one priest for every 781.

As noted earlier, the *OCD* did not report data on the Anointing of the Sick (formerly Last Rites) during this period. However, Fichter's one-year study of a parish in New Orleans provided some benchmark data. In a parish with 5,281 members, Fichter (1951, 123–35) recorded eighty-five funerals, including seventy-nine persons who received Last Rites (a ratio of one person receiving Last Rites for every sixty-seven parishioners).

The Late 1900s

In the past half century, anti-Catholicism has declined, and Catholics have moved from the bottom to the top and from the margins to the middle of American society (Davidson 2005; Pyle 2006). In the process, they have had fewer children and become less dependent on the Church. Moreover, the image of God as a harsh judge has been replaced by an image of God as an unconditional lover (Gallup and Castelli 1987, 15). According to Morris (1997, 356): "After Vatican II, notions of Hell, damnation, and mortal sin, almost overnight, virtually disappeared from the American Church." As a consequence, the laity now believes that its access to heaven has increased and that the likelihood of going to hell has diminished.

These conditions have led to lower rates of participation in most sacraments (see table 4.1). The Catholic population has grown from 46 million in 1965 (when the doors of immigration were reopened) to 64 million in

2005. Yet, no doubt reflecting the fact that Catholics are having fewer children than they used to, there has been an overall decline in the number of baptisms. In 1965, the Church recorded 1.4 million baptisms. In 2005, it recorded only one million. The ratio of baptisms to total Catholics has gone from one in thirty-three in 1965 to one in sixty-four in 2005.

Mass attendance reached all-time highs in the 1950s, with about three-quarters of Catholics going to Mass weekly or more, although considerably fewer went to Communion that often. By 1985, the weekly Mass attendance rate had slipped to 53 percent and the Communion rate to 39 percent (Gallup and Castelli 1987, 194–95). The Communion rate had climbed to 74 percent of the Mass attendance rate. Our 2005 survey indicates that about 34 percent of today's Catholics attend Mass weekly or more often. The percentage of Catholics receiving Holy Communion at least weekly is now about 83 percent of the weekly Mass attendance rate (Davidson 2005, 151). Clearly, today's Catholics do not attend Mass as often as they used to, but the vast majority of those who do go these days also go to Communion.

Because the *OCD* did not publish data on the number of Catholics who were confirmed each year until the 1980s, it is impossible to draw firm conclusions about long-term trends. Even so, a couple of comparisons can be made. For one, Fichter (1951) estimated that about half of eligible youth were confirmed in the mid-1940s. Hoge and his colleagues (2001, 40, 116–17) report that 30 to 40 percent of Hispanics and 60 to 70 percent of non-Hispanics are confirmed nowadays. Overall, these data suggest that the Confirmation rate may not have changed much over the years. More recent data of a different kind suggest much the same thing (see table 4.1). In 1995, the Church reported 576,887 confirmations (one for every ninety-nine Catholics). In 2005, it reported 610,282 (one for every 104 Catholics).

Next, we turn to the sacraments of vocation. First, marriage. Conflicting forces are affecting the statistics on the sacrament of Marriage. Although marriage is supposed to be a once-in-a-lifetime experience, an increasing number of Catholics have their marriages annulled and then "remarry" in the Church. On the other hand, Catholics are having smaller families, more and more Catholics are choosing not to marry at all, and an increasing number are choosing to marry outside the Church (recent survey data indicate that almost one-third of young adults are marrying under such circumstances [D'Antonio et al. 2001; Davidson 2005]). In that the *OCD* reports only the number of marriages that are witnessed each year by a priest (it does not include data on marriages in which a Catholic person or a Catholic couple is married "outside the Church"), the net effect is that the Church is reporting fewer and fewer marriages. After climbing to 355,182 in 1965, the number of marriages taking place in the Church declined quite steadily to only 207,112 in 2005. With the Catholic population rising and the number of marriages falling, the ratio of Church-approved marriages to total Catholics has risen from one in ninety-nine in 1945 to one in 323 in 2005.

Second, Holy Orders. The number of men being ordained to the priesthood is declining. It went from 1,118 in 1965 to 711 in 1985, to 583 in 1995, and to only 431 in 2004. As it did, the ratio of ordinations to Catholics also changed. It rose dramatically from one ordination per 41,365 Catholics in 1965 to one per 148,382 Catholics in 2005. As a result of declining ordinations (and increasing attrition), the total number of priests began to decline in the 1970s. By 1985, it had fallen to 57,183 (a ratio of one to 921). It had tumbled to 47,511 priests (and a ratio of one to 1,199) by 1995. In 2005, there were only 41,472 priests (one for every 1,542 Catholics).

The *OCD* does not report data on Catholics' participation in the sacrament of Reconciliation. However, a combination of earlier accounts and recent survey data give us a good idea of what the trend has been over the past fifty years or so. Consider Gillis's (1999, 169–70) account of what has taken place:

> In the 1950s and '60s, in any given parish three or four priests would hear confessions for several hours on Saturday afternoon and evening. Today, most parishes do not have the luxury of multiple priests and the small segment of the Catholic population (20 percent according to recent data) who go to confession regularly has eliminated the need for the parish priest to spend long hours in the confessional. In a previous era confessions would be heard every Saturday from perhaps 2 to 4 and 7 to 9 P.M.. Today parishes may regularly schedule the sacrament from 4:15 to 4:45 before the Saturday evening mass, and one priest can easily accommodate the small number of penitents, although Catholics are invited to contact a priest at other times if they wish to confess their sins and receive absolution.

Research by Fichter (1951, 55) and Greeley (1977, 127) shows that, in the 1950s and 1960s, about 80 percent of Catholics went to Confession at least once a year. By the 1970s, about 70 percent were doing so. The most recent survey data indicate that less than half of Catholics now make their "Easter duty." About 53 percent never go to Confession (Davidson 2005, 154–55).

Formerly known as "Extreme Unction" or "Last Rites," the sacrament now called the Anointing of the Sick is administered to dying persons, but it also is available to "all who are sick and who may need an additional sign and source of God's grace to cope with their illness, to be healed, to endure the suffering associated with illness" (Gillis 1999, 172). It is administered in hospitals, parishes, and private homes. Unfortunately, the Church does not record data on the number of people experiencing the

Anointing of the Sick, and we know of no recent research that gives any indication of how many people receive this sacrament each year.

SUMMATION

The data presented here point to enormous changes in Catholics' participation in the sacraments over the course of the past century or so. The overall pattern is like an inverted U-shaped curve, with relatively few Catholics participating in the early 1900s, many more doing so in the middle of the twentieth century, and fewer doing so in recent decades. This overall pattern is most definite with regard to Baptism, the Eucharist, and Holy Orders. The total number of baptisms increased through the middle of the century, then declined. Despite the influx of new, largely Catholic immigrants in recent decades, the number of baptisms has not kept up with the growth of the Catholic population. Church attendance and the reception of Communion also climbed through the middle of the century, but both have declined since then. The number of ordinations also increased then declined. The number of priests per Catholic increased through mid-century but has tapered off in recent decades.

The data are not quite as certain with regard to other sacraments. Part of the reason is that it is almost impossible to find long-term comparable data for the sacraments of Confirmation, Confession, Marriage, and the Anointing of the Sick. However, combining historical accounts and empirical data as best we can, it appears that the same inverted U-shaped pattern applies to at least two of these sacraments as well. The percentage of Catholics going to Confession regularly almost certainly peaked in the middle of the century before declining. So did the number of marriages recorded by the Church. The number of marriages obviously has not kept up with the total Catholic population in recent decades. The data on Confirmation point to more stability but are not as complete or reliable as we would like. There are only limited data relating to the Anointing of the Sick and none that would substantiate a long-term trend.

BELIEFS AND PRACTICES

All these developments led us to believe that the laity's interpretation of the sacraments would have changed considerably in recent years. We explored this possibility in our 2005 survey with regard to Catholics' understanding of the sacraments in general and two sacraments in particular: the Eucharist and Marriage (we offer a more extended analysis on Holy Orders in chapter

5). Let us begin by describing these views (see table 4.2), then we will explain the variations among the laity (tables 4.3, 4.4, and 4.5).

Describing Beliefs and Practices

Sacraments continue to be very important to American Catholics. According to our 2005 survey, three-quarters of Catholics say that sacraments such as the Eucharist are very important to them personally, 20 percent say that they are somewhat important, and 4 percent say that sacraments are unimportant. Eighty-one percent say that sacraments are essential to their relationship with God; only 17 percent disagree.

With regard to the Eucharist, two-thirds of Catholics say that one cannot be a good Catholic without believing that the bread and wine actually become the body and blood of Christ. Sixty percent say that reducing the number of Masses to fewer than once a week is an unacceptable response to the growing shortage of priests. Four in ten Catholics also say that having Communion services instead of Masses is unacceptable, yet 48 percent view this as somewhat acceptable. Although the Eucharist clearly is important to most Catholics, 76 percent believe that one can be a good Catholic without attending Mass on a weekly basis. It seems that laypeople distinguish between the value of the Eucharist (which they still accept) and the Church's rules governing access to it (which they do not seem to accept).

Three-quarters of married Catholics said their marriages had been approved by the Church as valid. However, two-thirds of Catholics also believe that one can be a good Catholic without having one's marriage approved by the Church and without obeying the Church's teaching on divorce and remarriage. Once again, Catholics seem to believe in the value of the sacrament, and a majority of laypeople continue to participate in it. However, they also believe that compliance with Church rules regarding marriage and divorce has little or nothing to do with one's status as a good Catholic.

Despite all of the recent turbulence in the Church, especially the sexual abuse scandal (see chapter 5), Catholics' attitudes about the sacraments have remained remarkably stable (see table 4.2). There have been no significant changes in Catholics' views relative to the Eucharist and marriage since our 1999 survey. It appears that Catholics' views about these sacraments have not been affected—one way or the other—by the sexual abuse scandal, which some have called the most traumatic crisis in American Catholic history.

Explaining Variations

Finally, we turn to the "why" question: Why are some Catholics in compliance with Church teachings about the sacraments and others are not?

Table 4.2. Catholics' Beliefs and Practices in Relation to the Sacraments, 1999 and 2005 (in percentages)

	1999 %	2005 %
Importance of sacraments		
Importance of the sacraments, such as the Eucharist		
Very	80	76
Somewhat	16	20
Not at all	4	4
The sacraments are essential to your relationship with God		
Strongly agree	—	52
Agree somewhat	—	29
Disagree	—	18
The Eucharist		
Mass attendance		
Weekly+	37	34
2–3 times per month	19	16
Once a month	14	14
Few times per year, seldom/never	29	36
Can be a good Catholic without going to Church every Sunday		
Yes	76	76
No	23	23
Can be a good Catholic without believing that in the Mass, the bread and wine actually become the body and blood of Christ		
Yes	38	36
No	60	63
Reducing the number of Mass to fewer than once a week		
Not at all acceptable	58	60
Somewhat acceptable	33	32
Very acceptable	9	8
Having a Communion service instead of a Mass some of the time[1]		
Not at all acceptable	—	39
Somewhat acceptable	—	48
Very acceptable	—	12
Marriage		
Marriage was approved by the Catholic Church as a valid marriage		
Yes	69	73
No	30	26
Can be a good Catholic without the marriage having been approved by the Church		
Yes	67	67
No	32	32
Can be a good Catholic without obeying the Church hierarchy's teaching on divorce and remarriage		
Yes	64	66
No	37	33

[1] In 1999, the question asked of Catholics was how often a Communion service would be acceptable. Twelve percent said "on a regular basis," 57 percent said "occasionally," and 30 percent said "not at all."

Church leaders and scholars have answered this question in different ways. Some have used "rational choice" theory. According to this approach, individuals calculate the costs and benefits of whatever options they face, avoiding the options whose costs outweigh the benefits and choosing the ones whose benefits outweigh the costs. This perspective suggests that Catholics participate in the sacraments and comply with Church teachings when it is in their interest to do so. When they have nothing to gain, they do not participate and they disagree with Church teachings. Finke and Stark (1992, 2000) have used this approach to explain recent trends in the Church, including the declining numbers of priests and sisters.

Our approach goes in a different direction. In contrast to rational choice theorists who emphasize the importance of self-interest, we emphasize the importance of self-concept. As we said it chapter 2, the term "self-concept" includes Catholics' identification with their faith and their attachment to the Catholic Church. We argue that these religious loyalties and attachments are shaped by the experiences they have during their formative years. Given the historical account we have provided, we expect that older Catholics belonging to the pre–Vatican II generation will be more attached to the faith and more in compliance with Church teachings than younger, post-Vatican II Catholics. But our emphasis is on the potency of religious identities and loyalties (that is, their ability to explain other beliefs and practices). In chapter 3, we showed that commitment to the Church is more consequential in Catholics' behavior than is identification with the faith. Thus, we hypothesize that highly committed Catholics are more likely to participate in the sacraments and to agree with Church teachings than Catholics who are only loosely connected to the Church.

Tables 4.3, 4.4, and 4.5 yield three conclusions that are consistent with our thesis. First, as we expected, Catholics' beliefs and practices are shaped by the experiences they have during their formative years. Pre–Vatican II Catholics are consistently more traditional in their outlook and their actions than are later generations. The post–Vatican II and Millennial generations are more likely to have attitudes and behaviors at odds with Church teachings related to the sacraments.

Second, commitment to the Church also is a strong predictor of Catholics' sacramental beliefs and practices. The more one is committed to the Church, the more likely one is to say that the sacraments are important and essential to one's relationship with God, that one cannot be a good Catholic without believing that in the Mass the bread and wine actually become the body and blood of Christ, that reducing the number of Masses to fewer than one a week is an unacceptable way of dealing with the priest shortage, that one had been married in the Church, that one cannot be a good Catholic without getting married in the Church, and that one cannot be a good Catholic without obeying Church teachings on divorce and remarriage.

Table 4.3. Influences on Catholic Attitudes toward the Sacraments, 2005 (in percentages)

	Sacraments Are	
	Very Important %	*Essential to My Relationship with God* %
Total	76	82
Church commitment		
High	100	99
Medium	77	82
Low	37	53
Generation		
Pre–Vatican II	81	89
Vatican II	76	81
Post–Vatican II	73	81
Millennial	77	76

Table 4.4. Influences on Catholic Attitudes toward the Eucharist, 2005 (percentage agreeing)

	Cannot be a good Catholic "without believing that in the Mass, the bread and wine actually become the body and blood of Jesus." %	*"Reducing the number of Masses to fewer than once a week" is "not at all acceptable."* %
Total	63	60
Church commitment		
High	79	73
Medium	62	58
Low	46	49
Generation		
Pre–Vatican II	65	60
Vatican II	65	58
Post–Vatican II	65	63
Millennial	45	51

Table 4.5. Influences on Catholic Attitudes toward Marriage, 2005 (percentage agreeing)

| | Cannot Be a Good Catholic | |
	"Without marriage being approved by the Church." %	"Without obeying teaching on divorce and remarriage." %
Total	32	33
Church commitment		
High	51	56
Medium	30	29
Low	16	16
Generation		
Pre–Vatican II	43	45
Vatican II	31	34
Post–Vatican II	31	29
Millennial	32	24

Third, of these two variables, commitment to the Catholic Church is a better predictor of belief and practice than is generation. The percentage differences between Catholics with high and low levels of commitment to the Church are larger than the differences between generations of Catholics.

CONCLUSION

The data in this chapter point to an inverted U-shaped trend in sacramental participation over time. Participation was uneven in the early 1900s, reached all-time highs in the 1950s, and dipped after that. These changes are best seen as adaptations to changing conditions in society and in the Church. In the 1950s, Protestant–Catholic tensions and Catholicism's image of God as a harsh judge fostered dependency on the Church and high levels of participation. Quite predictably, as Protestant–Catholic relations have improved and Catholics have come to see God as an unconditional lover who will forgive their sins, dependence on the Church and participation in the sacraments declined.

Catholics continue to see the sacraments as important, and they participate in them with noteworthy frequency, but they do so in varying degrees. These variations are closely tied to Catholics' commitment to the Church: the more Catholics are committed to the Church, the more they participate in the sacraments and the more traditional their beliefs tend to be. Commitment increases but does not guarantee compliance with Church teachings. Variations also are linked to generation, with pre–Vatican II Catholics being more involved and having more traditional views than younger Catholics. There are important differences within generations, but there also are central tendencies that go in different directions.

In the next chapter, we turn to Catholics' views of the problems facing the Catholic Church.

5

Problems Facing the Catholic Church

A reader of Catholic periodicals such as *First Things*, *Commonweal*, and *Liguorian* encounters numerous articles about problems facing the Church. One article will document the decline in Mass attendance over the past forty years. Another will examine the divisions between liberals and conservatives on issues such as abortion. Still another will insist that the bishops should do more to hold the line on core teachings of the Church.

If one listens to almost any group of Catholics talking about the Church these days—such as the mother–daughter conversation we have been recounting—one also will hear the same opinions. Somebody (like the mother) will complain about the poor quality of religious education in his or her parish. Somebody else (like the daughter) will bring up the sexual abuse scandal. Several people will express concern over the very future of the Church if the number of priests continues to decline the way it has for the past couple of decades. Yet another person will ask why today's young adults are not as involved in the Church as young adults used to be.

In short, Catholics are deeply concerned about a number of conditions in the Church. They are genuinely troubled by some past behavior, some current conditions, and some scary projections for the future. One goal of this chapter is to ascertain which problems laypeople consider to be the most serious. Related to this goal, we want to see how various subgroups of laypeople perceive these problems. For example, we want to find out how different generations of laypeople and Catholics with different levels of commitment to the Church interpret these problems.

THE MOST SERIOUS PROBLEMS

In 2003, we discussed these goals with several faculty and administrators at the University of Notre Dame. The group created a list of issues or problems that would reflect the concerns of various groups in the Church—men and women, older and younger Catholics, active and inactive Catholics, and liberals and conservatives. We inserted that list into the 2003 survey. A cross section of U.S. Catholics was asked to rate each issue as being "a serious problem," "somewhat of a problem," or "not a problem" (see figure 5.1). Here is what we found.

The sexual abuse scandal is seen as the main problem. The two facets of the scandal are both serious: that "some priests have sexually abused young people" (85 percent said it was serious) and that "some bishops have not done enough to stop priests from sexually abusing young people" (77 percent). But the laity have two other concerns as well. Sixty-two percent of Catholics say that "the shortage of priests and sisters" also is a serious problem. Next on the list was that "young adults are not involved in the Church as much as they should be," with 53 percent saying the situation is serious.

In the middle of the list are concerns that "parents don't teach their children the faith the way they should" (49 percent), "there are too many men with a homosexual orientation in the priesthood" (42 percent), "the Church's teachings on sexual morality are out of touch with reality today" (40 percent), and "women are not involved enough in Church decision making" (38 percent).

At the bottom of figure 5.1 are four issues that less than one-third of Catholics considered serious: that "laypeople are not consulted enough in forming the Church's moral and social teachings" (31 percent), that "laypeople no longer live up to the obligations involved in practicing the Catholic faith" (30 percent), that "there is poor religious education in parishes and Catholic schools" (27 percent), and that "bishops and priests no longer hold Catholics accountable to Church teachings" (25 percent). Although these problems are of major concern to some parents, theologians, and others in the Church, the laity as a whole is not nearly as troubled by them.

Thus, although laypeople are concerned about a number of problems, they seem to have a pretty clear sense of what the most important ones are: the sexual abuse scandal, the growing shortage of priests, and the relationship between young adult Catholics and the Church. In the rest of this chapter, we examine each of these issues. Other problems related to religious authority, church leadership, and religious education are discussed in chapters 6 and 7.

THE SEXUAL ABUSE SCANDAL

As early as the 1970s, there were occasional reports of priests abusing Catholic children, but most Catholics thought these were isolated cases. By the mid-1980s, more reports of such misconduct were appearing in the mass

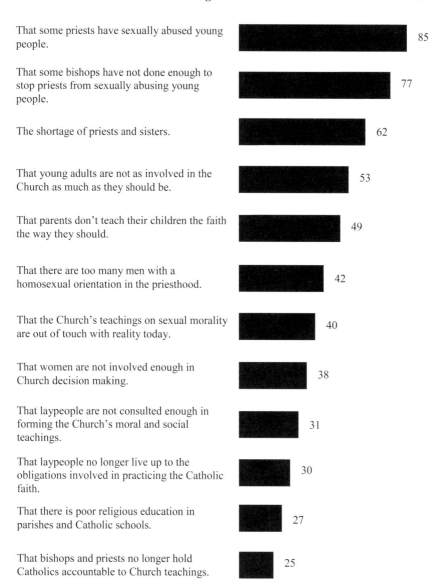

That some priests have sexually abused young people. 85

That some bishops have not done enough to stop priests from sexually abusing young people. 77

The shortage of priests and sisters. 62

That young adults are not as involved in the Church as much as they should be. 53

That parents don't teach their children the faith the way they should. 49

That there are too many men with a homosexual orientation in the priesthood. 42

That the Church's teachings on sexual morality are out of touch with reality today. 40

That women are not involved enough in Church decision making. 38

That laypeople are not consulted enough in forming the Church's moral and social teachings. 31

That laypeople no longer live up to the obligations involved in practicing the Catholic faith. 30

That there is poor religious education in parishes and Catholic schools. 27

That bishops and priests no longer hold Catholics accountable to Church teachings. 25

Figure 5.1. "How much of a problem is each of these twelve items—a serious problem, somewhat of a problem, or not a problem?" (percentage saying "a serious problem")

media. Bishops began to seek advice from medical experts as they sought remedies for what seemed to be a growing problem.

The situation worsened in the early 1990s. Father James Porter, Father Paul Shanley, and Father John Geoghan of Massachusetts and Father Bruce Ritter of New York were accused of sexual misconduct with young people and became nationally known symbols of the growing scandal. Cardinal Bernardin studied the problem in the Archdiocese of Chicago, learned how serious it was, and proposed a method for handling it. In June 1993, Peter Steinfels wrote an important article about the scandal in the *New York Times*. Other media—such as television (*60 Minutes*)—began to pay attention to the story as well.

All hell broke loose in January 2002 when the *Boston Globe* ran a series of stories on Father John Geoghan, the number of young people he had violated over the years, and Cardinal Law's practice of moving Geoghan from parish to parish without informing the laity of the priest's history. Other media leaped into the breach, conducting their own investigations and uncovering even more incidents of priests violating young Catholics. A year later, the *New York Times* estimated that 1,205 priests had been accused of sexual abuse since the 1930s. The Church then authorized investigations of its own, resulting in three reports in early 2004.[1] Those reports estimated that between 1950 and 2002, 4,392 priests had been accused of at least one credible incident of sexual immorality with 10,667 young people, mostly boys. Since then, additional cases have come to light. The latest estimate is that the scandal has cost the Church at least $1.5 billion (Filteau 2006). The fallout from the scandal continues as dioceses reduce chancery staffs, close parishes, sell off properties, and, in a few cases, declare bankruptcy.[2]

The Laity's Reactions

At the time of our 2003 survey, 91 percent of Catholics had heard about the sexual abuse scandal. Polls done by the Center for Applied Research in the Apostolate (CARA) between January 2002 and January 2006 also document the laity's awareness of the scandal. In 2006, 84 percent of Catholics

---

1. "Protecting God's Children: Report on the Implementation of the *Charter for the Protection of Children and Young People*" (Washington, D.C.: United States Conference of Catholic Bishops, December 2003); John Jay College of Criminal Justice, "The Nature and Scope of the Problem of Sexual Abuse of Minors by Catholic Priests and Deacons in the United States, 1950–2002" (Washington, D.C.: United States Conference of Catholic Bishops, February 2004); National Review Board, "Report on the Crisis in the Catholic Church in the United States" (Washington, D.C.: United States Conference of Catholic Bishops, February 2004).

2. For more details on and interpretations of the scandal, see Steinfels (2003), Gibson (2003), and Allen (2004).

said they paid at least "some attention" to the issue of sexual abuse in the Catholic Church (Gray and Perl 2006, 35). Between one-quarter and one-third of Catholics said they were aware of a priest in their diocese who had abused a child.

Of the respondents in the 2003 study who had heard of the scandal, 78 percent said they were "ashamed and embarrassed for my church" (see table 5.1). Seventy-two percent said that "the failure of bishops to stop the abuse is a bigger problem than the abuse itself." Two-thirds (66 percent) believe that "the cases that have been reported to date are only the tip of the iceberg." Clearly, laypeople feel ashamed, hold clergy accountable, and fear that the problem is deeper than it seems.

When we asked laypeople about the bishops' handling of the scandal, fully 62 percent said the bishops "are covering up the facts" (see table 5.1). Only 20 percent said the bishops "are being open and honest." The rest are not sure or believe that the situation involves some mixture of truth and cover-up. This finding alerts us to the level of skepticism many Catholics feel about the national leadership. Reestablishing their credibility is a major challenge facing the bishops.

CARA also has tracked the laity's perceptions of the way Church leaders have handled the scandal (Gray and Perl 2006). The percentage of laypeople saying that American bishops in general have done a "good" or

Table 5.1.   Lay Attitudes about Sexual Abuse by Priests, 2003 (percentage of those who have heard about the sexual abuse)

	%
Strongly agree or somewhat agree	
When I read reports about priests who sexually abused children, I am ashamed and embarrassed for my Church.	78
The failure of bishops to stop the abuse is a bigger problem than the abuse itself.	72
The media have prolonged the scandal by reporting the same stories over and over again.	69
The cases that have been reported to date are only the tip of the iceberg.	66
The media reports have been too anti-Catholic.	56
Are Church leaders being very open and honest about these sexual abuse cases, or are they covering up the facts?	
Being very open and honest	20
Covering up the facts	62
Some of both, don't know, or refused	18

"excellent" job started at only 34 percent in April 2002 and fell to 22 percent in May 2002. It increased to 36 percent by July 2003. Since then, it has fluctuated between 27 and 33 percent, where it stood in October 2005 (Gray and Perl 2006, 20). Laypeople have more positive perceptions of their own bishops and cardinals, with close to half saying that these leaders have done "good" or "excellent" work on the abuse issue. Laypeople increasingly believe that the scandal has "hurt the credibility of Church leaders who speak out on social or political issues." The percentage of laypeople saying that leaders' credibility has been hurt "a great deal" rose from 37 percent in October 2003 to 42 percent in September–October 2005 (Gray and Perl 2006, 25).

Impact

We also tried to assess the impact of the sexual abuse crisis on laypersons' own religious lives. Table 5.2 shows the impact on Church attendance, involvement in a parish, and financial contributions.

As has also been shown in recent studies by Foundations and Donors Interested in Catholic Affairs (FADICA), the scandal has had little overall

Table 5.2. Effect of Reports of Sexual Abuse on Laity, 2003 (percentage of those who have heard about the sexual abuse)

	%
Have these reports increased, decreased, or had no effect on your church attendance?	
Increased	7
Decreased	11
No effect	78
Have these reports increased, decreased, or had no effect on your involvement in a parish?	
Increased	7
Decreased	10
No effect	80
Have these reports increased, decreased, or had no effect on your financial contributions to the Church?	
Increased	6
Decreased	12
No effect	80

Note: "Don't know" is not shown.

effect on laypeople's participation in the Church. About 80 percent of Catholics who attend Mass on a regular basis report that the scandal has had no effect on their frequency of attendance at Mass, involvement in parish activities, and financial contributions. But the scandal has affected the thoughts and actions of the other 20 percent. Not surprisingly, it has reduced some Catholics' participation. Unexpectedly, it has increased the participation of some others (we examine these variations later).

Although 78 percent of American Catholics said it had "no effect" on their Church attendance, 11 percent said their attendance had decreased, and 7 percent said it had increased. When asked about the scandal's impact on their parish involvement, 80 percent said "no effect," 10 percent reported a decline, and 7 percent noted an increase. Eighty-one percent said their financial contributions had not changed, 12 percent reported a decrease, and 6 percent reported an increase.

These findings are consistent with FADICA's data indicating that the net effect of the scandal has been only a slight reduction in Catholics' participation and religious giving. The overall picture is one of stability, not decline, although there is more decline in places such as Boston.[3]

Variations

Clearly, laypeople were appalled by the behavior of priests who have abused young Catholics and especially by the way the bishops have handled the whole situation. People at all levels of commitment to the Church and in all four generations viewed the priests' behavior as a serious problem (see table 5.3).

They also saw the bishops' handling of the problem as a serious problem itself (see table 5.4). But laypeople varied in their views of the bishops' actions. Nonparishioners and infrequent Mass attenders were more likely to see the bishops' actions as a problem than were parishioners and weekly churchgoers. Pre–Vatican II Catholics were slightly more likely than younger Catholics to feel ashamed by the scandal (85 versus 76 percent for the Millennials and 74 percent for the post–Vatican II generation). Younger Catholics were more likely to think that the reported cases are just the tip of the iceberg (66 percent of the Millennials and 74 percent of post–Vatican II Catholics versus 48 percent of older Catholics). Thus, older Catholics were the most offended, but younger Catholics were more concerned that the worst might not be over.

In short, all indications are that the sexual abuse scandal is at the top of

---

3. The estimated $1.5 billion impact of the scandal has hit hardest the archdioceses of Boston and Los Angeles, along with the dioceses of Covington and Louisville, Kentucky (see *National Catholic Reporter*, April 28, 2006).

Table 5.3.   Views of Priests' Abuse of Children, by Commitment and Generation: Degree of Seriousness, 2003

	Very Serious %	Somewhat Serious %	Not Serious %	Don't Know, No Response %
Total sample	85	11	2	4
Commitment				
Parishioners	82	12	2	4
Nonparishioners	88	8	2	2
Attend weekly +	83	11	2	5
2–3 times per month	86	9	2	2
About once per month	82	12	3	3
Less than once a month	87	10	1	2
Generation				
Pre–Vatican II	86	10	—	4
Vatican II	85	11	1	3
Post–Vatican II	85	11	2	1
Millennial	81	7	5	6

Table 5.4.   Views of Bishops' Handling of Abuse Cases, by Commitment and Generation: Degree of Seriousness, 2003

	Very Serious %	Somewhat Serious %	Not Serious %	Don't Know, No Response %
Total sample	77	15	3	5
Commitment				
Parishioners	74	17	3	6
Nonparishioners	81	12	2	4
Attend weekly +	74	17	3	7
2–3 times per month	80	11	5	4
About once per month	77	17	3	3
Less than once a month	82	12	2	5
Generation				
Pre–Vatican II	75	15	2	8
Vatican II	80	12	3	5
Post–Vatican II	78	16	2	4
Millennial	70	18	5	6

most Catholics' list of problems that the Church needs to resolve. Laypeople have been shocked and outraged by the actions of those priests who have violated young people, but they are equally upset by the bishops' mishandling of the abuses. Through it all, however, the laity have demonstrated remarkable perseverance. Eighty percent of laypeople have continued to participate in the Church in much the same way that they did prior to the scandal. Among the other 20 percent, the scandal has dampened participation a bit more than it has enhanced it.

PRIEST SHORTAGE

In chapter 4, we described the growing shortage of priests in the United States. The Catholic population of the United States rose from 29 million in 1950 to 64 million in 2005. The number of priests fell from 43,889 to 41,472 over the same period of time. As the number of Catholic laypeople continues to increase and total number of priests continues to fall, the priest shortage will become even more severe in the years ahead. Given the crucial link between priests and the availability of the sacraments to the laity, we wondered how laypeople viewed the priest shortage.

Laity's Interpretations of the Priest Shortage

As one might expect, Catholics with the highest levels of involvement were more likely than less committed Catholics to see the priest shortage as a problem (see table 5.5). Two-thirds of parishioners, compared with just over half of nonparishioners, said it was a serious problem. Weekly Mass attenders were much more likely to say so than people who attend Mass less often.

Catholics' views about the priest shortage also were closely tied to generation. As one might expect, pre–Vatican II Catholics are most likely to see the priest shortage as a serious problem (78 percent). After all, they grew up in a Church that had an abundance of priests. They have a hard time imagining how the Church could survive with very few priests. Two-thirds of Vatican II Catholics and 58 percent of the post–Vatican II generation also think that the priest shortage is serious. The Millennial generation, which has grown up with many fewer priests, is the least likely to view the shortage as serious.

Expanding the Pool

The Church is trying to expand the pool of potential priests in several ways. Bishops and pastors frequently ask laypeople to pray for more voca-

Table 5.5.   View of Priest Shortage, by Commitment and Generation: Degree of
Seriousness, 2003

	Very Serious %	Somewhat Serious %	Not Serious %	Don't Know, No Response %
Total sample	62	24	8	7
Commitment				
Parishioners	68	23	4	4
Nonparishioners	52	24	14	9
Attend weekly +	71	19	5	5
2–3 times per month	67	18	9	6
About once per month	54	35	3	8
Less than once a month	45	31	14	10
Generation				
Pre–Vatican II	78	14	4	4
Vatican II	66	24	5	5
Post–Vatican II	58	25	10	7
Millennial	41	33	17	9

tions. Catholic parents are often urged to ask their sons to consider the priesthood. Long-standing groups, such as the Serra Club, are redoubling their efforts to recruit more men to seminaries. Whatever the merit and effect of these efforts might be, at least to date, they have not resulted in any reversal of the shortage. Seminary enrollments continue to decline.

The Church has not formally considered the possibility of expanding eligibility for the priesthood. Pope John Paul II would not entertain this possibility. Pope Benedict XVI allowed some discussion of it at the 2005 Synod of Bishops, but it did not gain the support of a majority of bishops, so it is not receiving any further attention at this time. Still, studies have shown that laypeople are thinking about this possible course of action. There are several possibilities, including the ordination of married men, the ordination of women, and accepting resigned priests who have married back into active priestly ministry. Questions about whether lay Catholics would accept these options have been included in various surveys for three decades (see table 5.6). Acceptance of married priests increased from 63 percent in 1987 to 75 percent in 2005. In the 1999 survey, we added a statement: "It would be a good thing if priests who have married were allowed to return to active ministry." Agreement with this statement increased from 77 percent in 1999 to 81 percent in 2005, and it is the most acceptable of all the options in the table.

On the question of women priests, we have longer-trend survey data.

Table 5.6. Catholics' Agreement with Possible Responses to the Priest Shortage, 1985–2005

"It would be a good thing if . . ."	1985 %	1993 %	1999 %	2005 %
Married men were allowed to be ordained	63	72	71	75
Priests who have married were returned to active ministry	—	—	77	81
Celibate women were allowed to be ordained as priests	—	—	63	61
Married women were allowed to be ordained as priests	—	—	54	54

Catholics have greatly increased their support for having women priests since the earliest survey in 1974. Beginning in 1999, we distinguished between ordaining celibate women and married women. More Catholics are in favor of celibate women priests than married women priests, although a majority of Catholics favor both. The laypeople with whom we have spoken seem to favor the ordination of women religious most of all.

When we looked more closely at the characteristics of the Catholics who support ordaining married men, we found some interesting differences. The most highly committed Catholics are less likely than others to agree to ordaining married men. Women are more supportive than men of ordaining married men, and the post–Vatican II generation is more supportive than the older generations. People with an income under $75,000 are more supportive than those earning more, and those who attend Mass less than weekly are more supportive than weekly attenders.

The priest shortage will be with us for some time to come. Catholics will have to cope with it in their parishes in whatever ways they can. In chapter 7, we explore some of the methods that are being considered or that are already being implemented in several places.

YOUNG ADULTS AND THE CHURCH

In the 2003 survey, just over half of American Catholics said that young adults' lack of participation in the Church is a serious problem. We also found that older Catholics were more likely than younger Catholics were to view it as a serious problem (see table 5.7). Fifty-eight percent of pre–Vatican II Catholics and 57 percent of Vatican II Catholics saw a serious problem. Less than half of post–Vatican II and Millennial Catholics did.[4]

---

4. Parishioners were as likely as nonparishioners to say that young adults' lack of participation in the Church is a serious problem. Regular Mass attenders and less frequent churchgoers also had similar views on this issue.

Table 5.7.　Views of Lack of Young Adult Church Participation, by Commitment and Generation: Degree of Seriousness, 2003

	Very Serious %	Somewhat Serious %	Not Serious %	Don't Know, No Response %
Total sample	53	34	9	4
Commitment				
Parishioners	53	37	7	3
Nonparishioners	53	30	11	4
Attend weekly +	56	34	7	3
2–3 times per month	58	32	8	2
About once per month	38	48	10	4
Less than once a month	50	32	11	7
Generation				
Pre–Vatican II	58	29	5	7
Vatican II	57	28	10	5
Post–Vatican II	48	40	10	2
Millennial	48	43	5	3

We should not be surprised. After all, older people have always viewed young people as a problem. Mary and Joseph were upset when their unruly son, Jesus, wandered off to the temple without telling them where he was going. When they found and chastised him, he was not contrite. Rather, he confronted his parents.

In the play and movie *Fiddler on the Roof*, a nineteenth-century Eastern European Jewish father (Tevya) struggled with the fact that his daughters did not embrace Jewish traditions as fully as he thought they should. They were not willing to settle for the men their elders had decided they should marry. His anguish was clearly evident in his heart-wrenching song about the loss of the Jewish tradition as he knew it.

In the 1950s and 1960s, American parents who loved the big-band sounds of musicians such as Glenn Miller, Count Basie, and Les and Larry Elgart grimaced as their young adult offspring turned their backs on that musical genre and opted, instead, for rock 'n' roll: Elvis, Bill Haley and the Comets, and the Beatles. But music was only one expression of the "generation gap" of that period. Young adults of that time were deliberately countercultural in many ways. Much to their parents' chagrin, many of them criticized religion and other institutions, opposed the Vietnam War, did drugs, celebrated "free love," and questioned all kinds of authority.

So, in some sense, there is nothing new under the sun. We have always had a generation gap. Parents will always use the criteria of their generation to judge their children, who belong to a different generation. The children, in turn, will reject their parents' criteria and resent the negative parental view of them and their behavior. They will prefer to be seen as important in their own right and will want to be judged by criteria that apply to their own generation, not someone else's.

Yet the ubiquity of a generation gap does not diminish the importance of the problems it poses for families and religious groups. There is a need to understand the relationship between the Church and today's young adults.

The Relationship between the Church and Young Adults as Older Catholics See It

Older, pre–Vatican II Catholics grew up in times when there was an emphasis on one's responsibility to obey both secular and religious authority. There was a strong sense of duty to comply with the expectations of one's superiors. There was a distinct sense of obligation to group norms and values. As young adults in the 1930s and 1940s, pre–Vatican Catholics had been expected to be actively involved in the Church, and all indications are that they were. Research showed that most young adult Catholics in that era attended Mass on a weekly basis, received Holy Communion after going to Confession, and married in the Church. Not all young Catholics complied with Church teachings, but most conformed (Davidson et al. 1997, 16–20).

As parents, members of the pre–Vatican II generation expected their children to do the same. For the most part, their children did. Although the young adults of the 1950s and 1960s were not as attached as their parents to the Church, all indications are that they were still quite involved. For example, about 70 percent of all Catholics and a majority of young adult Catholics attended Mass every Sunday (Greeley 1977, 127; Lenski 1961, 37; Stark and Glock 1968, 83–86).

By the mid- to late 1960s, American society was putting more emphasis on a voluntaristic view of one's relationship to all kinds of institutions, including the Church. In addition, Church leaders were urging laypeople to take personal responsibility for their own "faith journey." These forces combined to reduce Catholics' sense of obligation to obey Church rules and regulations. Mass attendance—and Church participation generally—began to decline. That trend has continued to the point that only 34 percent of all Catholics and only one-quarter of young adults in our 2005 survey attended Mass weekly.

Older Catholics have watched as Church participation rates have gone down. They have known a past when young adults were highly involved in the Church, and they see that this is no longer true. They fear that, without active young people, the Church's future might be in jeopardy. It is a fear linked to two other items in figure 5.1: the concern that today's parents no longer educate their children in the faith the way parents used to (see the fifth item) and the concern about the quality of religious education programs in parishes and parochial schools (the second-to-last item). Older Catholics were more likely than younger Catholics to see these as problems.

Pre–Vatican II and Vatican II Catholics grew up in an era when priests and nuns took the lead in teaching young people the fundamentals of the faith. The preferred method of learning at the time was memorization. Catholics who grew up in that era vividly recall the strictness of the priests and sisters who insisted that they memorize the questions and answers in the *Baltimore Catechism* and the swiftness of the punishment these educators delivered when students failed to do so. Although parents could not always explain the specifics of the faith to their children, they reinforced the priests' and sisters' efforts to do so by monitoring their children's homework. Many parents read the questions and asked their children for the answers on Saturday night or early Sunday morning—to make sure they knew the answers before going to class.

Older Catholics sense that today's religious educators are more focused on process than content. They hear of Confraternity of Christian Doctrine (CCD) projects in which youngsters spend more time drawing pictures or creating posters than they do learning the Ten Commandments or the Beatitudes. They also know of parents who do not participate in their children's religious education the way previous generations of parents did. There are widely circulated stories of parents who drop their kids off at CCD, go to a nearby coffee shop instead of Mass, and come back to pick up their kids an hour later. Older Catholics' suspicions about the mediocrity of some of today's religious education and parents' lack of attention to their children's religious formation are bolstered by reports from professors of theology indicating that today's young adults do not understand some of the basic tenets of the Catholic faith.

The Relationship as Young Adults See It

Young adults in our 2003 survey were not as likely to see their relationship to the Church as problematic—and for good reason. Like any generation of young adults, they tend to have a positive view of themselves. In our interactions and conversations with young adults, we found that they have a number of attributes. These include the following:

- Extraordinary computer skills that members of older generations often lack
- More tolerance of racial, ethnic, and religious diversity than older Catholics
- Great imaginations and a keen sense of irony

- An emphasis on personal fulfillment (they want meaningful work, not dead-end jobs)
- A desire to postpone marriage until they have established careers and can make mature decisions about a spouse and family
- A knack for seeing gaps between words and deeds (they can't stand hypocrisy)
- An ability to combine sacred and secular symbols
- Belief in a personal God, who is an important part of their lives and with whom they talk on a fairly regular basis
- Agreement with core Church teachings, such as the Incarnation, the Resurrection, Jesus' Real Presence in the Eucharist, and Mary as the Mother of God
- A belief that being Catholic has to do with the way we treat others, especially the poor

But there is more to it than just feeling good about your generation. In contrast to earlier generations of young adult Catholics, who were taught to obey secular and religious authorities, today's young adults have been taught to think for themselves (Alwin 1984, 1986). They also have been taught to take responsibility for their own relationship with God (Davidson 2005). Following these guidelines, young adults differentiate between beliefs and practices they consider central to the faith and ones they consider peripheral or optional (Hoge et al. 2001). As long as they believe in God, Jesus' Incarnation and Resurrection, and Mary as the Mother of God and as long as they do whatever they can to love their neighbor, they do not feel obliged to attend Mass every week, go to Confession every year, or even marry in the Church. As a result, they continue to see themselves as spiritual, and they participate in the Church when they are in the right frame of mind. Although their rate of participation is lower than that of their parents' and grandparents' generations, they view it as quite natural. They do not see it as a serious matter.

Moreover, a sizable minority of young adults are very spiritual and highly religious. As Colleen Carroll has shown in her book *The New Faithful*, a sizable number of young adults—we estimate about 20 percent—attend Mass and go to Communion regularly, go to Confession occasionally, think of themselves as "orthodox" Christians, and read the scriptures whenever they can. They are very concerned about the poor and the vulnerable, expressing what many of them consider the very heart of Christ's gospel. Some are considering the priesthood or life as women religious; others are planning to marry in the Church, raise their kids in the Church, and dedicate their lives to Jesus Christ. They see themselves as the future of the Church and are quite naturally offended when others describe young adults as a problem.

Yet nearly half of the young adults in our 2003 survey said their generation's relationship to the Church is a serious problem. What are they point-ing to? Our recent studies provide several clues. For one thing, many young adults feel they were never taught the basic truths of the Catholic faith. In books like *The Search for Common Ground* (Davidson et al. 1997) and *Young Adult Catholics* (Hoge et al. 2001), young adults assert that their religious educations included a lot of process but not a lot of content. Some com-plain that more time was spent in making collages than in listening to explications of fundamental Church teachings. Others say they enjoyed their service-learning experiences working with the poor but regret that they do not understand their faith enough to explain it to their children.

Other young adults are troubled by the discrepancy between Church teachings on sexual and reproductive issues and their own views on topics such as artificial birth control, abortion, homosexuality, and the ordination of women and married men (Hoge et al. 2001). It is unlikely that the Church will change its views on these issues any time soon. Nor are post–Vatican II and Millennial Catholics likely to change their views. Thus, young adults—more than older Catholics—are faced with participating in an institution that does not reflect their worldview. The Church also is con-fronted with ministering to young adults who disagree with many of its policies and practices.

There also are generational tensions around the salience of key issues. Many older members of the Church hierarchy seem more concerned about personal moral issues (especially abortion), and many young adults attach higher priority to social issues (such as the sources and consequences of poverty). Indeed, at a time when some key figures in the Church are tending to define Catholic orthodoxy in terms of compliance with the Church's sex-ual teachings, young Catholics seem more inclined to define it in terms of social service and social justice (Hoge et al. 2001). These tensions pose seri-ous problems for both young adults and the Church.

Finally, as young adults move into the ranks of the most educated and most prosperous generation of Catholics in the history of the Church, they express a desire to be actively involved in all phases of Church life (D'An-tonio et al. 2001). Yet, with increased frequency, they encounter priests who do not wish to share authority with laypeople (Hoge and Wenger 2003). The relationship between young adults and the Church hangs in the bal-ance.

Evidence of a Tenuous Relationship

There is considerable evidence of the tenuous nature of the relationship between the institutional Church and today's young adults. Putnam's research on Americans' participation in voluntary associations shows that—compared with young adults in earlier generations—today's young adults are less attached to all sorts of social institutions, including churches (Putnam 2000). In line with Putnam's thesis, chapter 3 showed that younger Catholics' levels of commitment to the Church fall short of their parents. On our three-item index of commitment, we found that 43 percent of pre–Vatican II Catholics but only 20 percent of Vatican II Catholics, 17 percent of post–Vatican II Catholics, and none of the Millennial Catholics scored high. Moreover, as we showed in chapter 2, post–Vatican II and Millennial Catholics were somewhat less likely than members of older generations to identify with the Catholic faith, embrace core Church teachings, and stress the distinctiveness of Catholicism relative to other faiths. By these measures—all of which involve comparisons with previous generations—young adults' relationship to the Church is problematic.

But even if we avoid such comparisons with older generations and focus just on today's young adults, the evidence suggests that young adults are only loosely tethered to the Church. Barely half say they would never leave the Church. Only four in ten say the Church is the most important part—or one of the most important parts—of their lives. Only one-fourth go to Mass on a weekly basis. Less than half believe that the teaching authority claimed by the Vatican is very important. A majority disagree with Church teachings related to sexual and reproductive issues, such as birth control and abortion. A majority also reject some of the Church's key social teachings, such as its opposition to capital punishment. And if a sizable number of young adults report that they do not understand their faith well enough to explain it to their own children, they have a problem, and so does the Church.

CONCLUSION

Catholics are concerned about many issues facing their Church. Chief among them are the sexual abuse scandal, the priest shortage, and the link between young adults and the Church. Older and more committed Catholics are a bit more likely to be troubled by these issues than younger and less committed Catholics, but there is widespread agreement that these problems need to be addressed. Implicit in our findings is a concern that if these problems are not addressed, the Church's future might be in jeopardy.

These three issues—and several others on our list of twelve topics—raise a number of questions about the nature and use of authority in the Church. Because the matter of authority cuts across so many issues, we pay special attention to it in our next chapter.

6

American Catholics and Church Authority

One of the goals of our surveys has been to describe the way American Catholics relate to the formal teaching authority of the Catholic Church. The Church's teaching authority covers a broad range of moral and structural issues; some of the moral issues concern family and human sexuality, others concern war and capital punishment, and still others concern social justice for the poor, aged, and persons otherwise neglected in human society. Structural issues have to do with the Church's hierarchic governing structure and access to roles within it (Casanova 1994; Gibson 2003; Oakley and Russett 2004; Steinfels 2003).

The roots of the Catholic Church's claims to authority are found in the Gospels and the writings of Peter, Paul, and other apostles, often based on their own firsthand experiences with Jesus. As the centuries passed, the Church developed its teachings, beginning with the definitive teachings that emerged from the Council of Nicaea (325 C.E.), commonly known as the Creed. Church authority was also built on its claims to apostolic succession, in this case citing the passage from the Gospel of Matthew, "Upon this rock [Peter], I will build my church" (Matthew 16:18). In its most formal sense, the Church's claims to authority rest on the scriptures, apostolic succession, and tradition (Noonan 2005).

---

1. *Governance, Accountability, and the Future of the Catholic Church*, an edited book derived from a conference held at the Yale Law School in March 2003, recognizes that the current crisis in the Church is part of a larger crisis that has brought "into question all forms of authority, secular no less than ecclesiastical." It addresses such central questions as 1) the historical antecedents to the contemporary hierarchical and centralized institution that is the Church; 2) relevant theological perspectives on greater responsibility for the laity and clergy; 3) existing models of structures that would create greater participation and accountability, including financial accountability; and 4) features from the American experience of freedom and democracy

All indications from social research are that acceptance of the Catholic Church's moral authority has been diminishing since Vatican II.[1] To understand why this may be so, we look at the nature of authority in general and how it rises or falls throughout historical periods.

MEASURING AUTHORITY

The most quoted sociological definition of authority is Max Weber's: "the probability that certain specific commands from a given source will be obeyed by a given group of persons" (1947, 324). This kind of *authority* refers specifically to voluntary obedience, in contrast to *coercion*, which connotes nonvoluntary obedience. Thus, the legitimacy of a leader's commands rests in the voluntary nature of the obedience of the followers.

Authority entails not merely a proclamation by a leader but also the probability that a follower or group of followers will accept the proclamation and obey it. Thus, authority becomes fully legitimate when it is claimed by a leader or office (in this case the papacy) and the claim is accepted by the follower or followers (the bishops and the laity). In a free and democratic society, the legitimacy of authority ultimately rests in the hands of followers, who make their own decisions on the basis of their perceptions of the leader, the office held by the leader, and the leader's justification for the claim. This is called rational-legal authority, and it is the foundation on which democratic society is based. Although the Catholic Church in the United States has become more and more a voluntary association as people choose to affiliate or leave, by its own admission it is grounded more in traditional than in rational-legal authority and is not a democratic organization in any sense in which that term has current meaning.

In earlier times in Catholic countries, religious claims were often backed by political force. To the extent that physical or psychological forms of coercion were used, the claimed authority lacked legitimacy even though large numbers of Catholics may have acquiesced at least overtly. But today in Western societies, religious leaders cannot use force. They can only ask for voluntary obedience. The followers will obey the teachings if they believe that the teachings are legitimate, justified, and true to the will of God as they understand that will. If the followers doubt the claims for whatever

---

that might prove either helpful or hurtful in efforts to encourage participation. The book is a clarion call for voice from those whose loyalty to the Church in crisis means "speaking up, insisting on being heard and heeded," acknowledging that action for change "requires a long-sustained effort" (Oakley and Russett 2004, 201–2).

reason, including their own consciences, they will feel free to follow their consciences as having supremacy over obedience.

In today's world, where claims of authority are expounded daily by all kinds of leaders and "wannabe" leaders, even within the Catholic Church, there is a growing gap between claims to authority and accepted authority. More authority is claimed than is accepted. To estimate the gap, one needs to know as much as possible about both claimed and accepted authority. In the case of the Catholic Church today, the claims to authority are found in the Catechism of the Catholic Church, the encyclical letters of the popes, and the writings and public statements of the bishops. Theologians and philosophers may prepare formal statements for official use by popes and bishops, but the formal authority statements come from the bishops themselves.

For centuries, the hierarchy attended to its teaching responsibility by adhering to a monarchical style of leadership and governance relying on a mix of traditional authority and deductive reasoning (Beal 2004; Colish 2004). It developed moral positions deductively and disseminated them downward. The hierarchy in Rome and in local dioceses worked through the structures of parishes, schools, and other institutions to promulgate Church policies and doctrines to the laity. Letters from Rome or from the local bishop were regularly read at Mass, and students at all levels of schooling were taught the Church's position on moral issues.

But the Catholic Church was beset during the nineteenth and early twentieth centuries by events introduced by modern life (Fogarty 2004). The worldwide spread of democratic civil governance was accompanied by the gradual extension of suffrage to women, blacks, and other oppressed peoples. As a result, more people than ever, including Catholics, became accustomed to being part of decision-making structures, built on rational-legal authority. The dramatic growth in formal education, especially in the United States after World War II, enabled people to become more informed about issues affecting their lives, further undercutting systems of hierarchical, tradition-oriented governance. Administrative requirements for running bureaucracies, such as the need for input from accountants and financial advisers, made it difficult for a church elite to govern without consulting with laity. Premises of traditional Church teachings were challenged by demographic trends, such as decreased fertility and increasing longevity. The fact that women, in particular, could expect to spend a significant portion of their lives without parenting responsibilities raised questions about the association between sex and family life. While Catholics continued to maintain strong ties to family and church, they were also becoming more and more a part of American society with its emphasis on personal autonomy.

These experiences underscored the importance of certain values and their potential conflict with others. Catholics' success within a structure of religious pluralism supported principles of religious tolerance (Murray 1960), challenging the mentality that had dominated the hierarchy for more than a century. Norms of self-fulfillment and individuals' rights burgeoned. As Greeley (1973) noted, the emphasis on personal autonomy was one of the century's most important cultural developments. Professionalism and expertise gained in importance. A steadily growing population of Catholics was also becoming mainstream American. When John XXIII succeeded Pius XII in 1958, American Catholics were ready to heed his call to open the windows of the Church and let in some fresh air.

Pope John XXIII wanted Vatican Council II to revitalize and update the Church, to bring it into the modern world. From 1962 to 1965, the Council did so, as the body of more than 2,000 bishops found middle ways between the most progressive and the most traditional forces. The Council, in its documents, reaffirmed the joint authority of the bishops with the pope; it opened a biblical perspective toward the Church; it made important changes in the liturgy, especially the use of the vernacular in the Mass; it encouraged ecumenical activity; it fostered episcopal leadership; for the first time it emphasized the importance of conjugal love in marriage; it heralded freedom of religion and conscience; it encouraged active engagement with the larger social world; and it gave new emphasis to the laity as "the people of God, the body of Christ, and a community of faith." And most important, by all accounts these new teachings were widely accepted by the great majority of the American laity (Greeley et al. 1976).

In retrospect, the tumult in the wake of Vatican II should not have been surprising. Yet the social structures needed to implement the changes made by the Council were lacking. The documents themselves did not provide more than a general idea about how to bring about structural changes. On matters of moral authority, laypeople were encouraged to believe that they had freedom of conscience. For them, this has come to mean combining reason, faith, and experience to reach decisions on a wide range of moral issues (Dillon 1999). The outcome of the tension between obedience and conscience was predicted forty years ago: "In the long run the laity will do what seems rational and practical, and whenever the Church is defending a tradition that cannot be sustained by reason, it will probably be ignored" (D'Antonio 1966, 12).

We will always be left to wonder what might have been had the encyclical *Humanae Vitae* incorporated the recommendation for change made by the great majority of the Papal Birth Control Commission rather than the reaffirmation of the traditional teaching by the minority that it did. The debate over birth control—and especially over the birth control pill—had become very public in the United States during the period from 1960 to 1968, and American Catholics had come to expect a change in Church teachings. No event of the twentieth century so challenged the teaching authority of the

Vatican as the debate about birth control and the publication of the encyclical (Bianchi and Ruether 1992; Dolan 1987; Fox 1995; Greeley 1977, 1979; Greeley et al. 1976; Wills 2000). For the great majority of Catholics, Vatican II was a positive change, bringing the Church closer to the modern world with its emphasis on rational authority and personal responsibility. In contrast, *Humanae Vitae* was seen as contradictory of the more open and self-responsible Catholicism. It was rejected by a majority of the laity and by a large number of priests and theologians. The U.S. bishops stood firmly with Rome; bishops in other countries took a variety of stands, some firmly with Rome, others citing the need to inform and follow one's conscience (Coffey 1998; Greeley 1990).

THE GROWING SPLIT BETWEEN
CONSERVATIVE AND PROGRESSIVE CATHOLICS

The previously mentioned historical overview outlines some of the major events that have helped to undermine what was until Vatican II a largely unchallenged Church teaching authority. In the four decades since *Humanae Vitae*, there has emerged a spectrum of groups among American Catholics. On the far right is a conservative group, often identifying its position as being the only properly orthodox Catholic position as it "emphasizes the stability of the institutional Church. This group is concerned about the credibility of the Church and its persistence as a social institution. It is rooted in the traditional, hierarchical exercise of authority" (Kennedy 1988). Its position is exemplified by the Reverend John Ford, one of the moral theologians on the Papal Birth Control Commission who was one of the four dissenters from the commission's report in 1965. He defended the Church's teaching on the evil of contraception in these words:

> The church cannot change her answer because this answer is true. . . . It is true because the Catholic Church, instituted by Christ to show men a secure way to eternal life, could not have so wrongly erred during all those centuries of history. . . . The Church could not have erred . . . even through one century, by imposing under serious obligation very grave burdens in the name of Jesus Christ, if Jesus Christ did not actually impose those burdens. . . . If the Church could err in such a way . . . the faithful could not put their trust in the magisterium's presentation of moral teaching especially in sexual matters. (cited in McClory 1995, 110–11)

On the other end of the spectrum are the progressive Catholics. According to Kennedy, they reflect the modern world with its emphasis on personal autonomy. They believe that the locus of authority is within the believer—that God speaks through the experiences and reflections of individual Christians. From this perspective, Catholics must take personal responsibility for the faith and for living that faith in the world. This understanding of the Catholic faith in the modern world was contained in advice given by married Catholics in the Christian Family Movement to the Papal Birth Control Commission in 1965:

> God has created us to develop our talents to govern the universe and ourselves. Since medical research has learned a method of intelligently controlling ovulation, it would seem reasonable for men to use this knowledge for the good of their own family. Other functions are intelligently controlled with no question as to the morality of the use of a drug. (McClory 1995, 94)[2]

The reality of American Catholics is that the groups at each end of the continuum are small, with a majority of Catholics in the middle. In a test of Kennedy's thesis, Davidson and Pogorelc found a majority of American Catholics (52 percent) in the middle, 12 percent on the conservative side, and 35 percent on the progressive side (Davidson 2005).

MEASURING THE ACCEPTANCE OF CLAIMS TO AUTHORITY

Is the Church's authority being accepted by Catholics today? To measure the level of accepted authority is a different kind of task from finding and describing the Church's teachings, which are found in the Catechism, encyclicals, and pastoral letters. Measuring accepted authority requires empirical measures of the degree to which followers accept the teachings or commands.

Claims for authority may be either institutional or personal. A leader may demand obedience based on his or her office or on personality or charisma. Catholic leaders normally depend on the authority of office and remind the faithful of the institution's history, traditions, and past claims to legitimacy. When that is sufficient to induce obedience, the authority of leaders has been strong, predictable, and stable. But if the followers lose faith in the institution, any authority based on Church office or tradition becomes shaky.

---

2. On the other hand, Dulles (1998) argued that the cultural secularization that has created the progressive Catholicism has put Catholic orthodoxy under enormous pressure. He accepted that "in a secularized society such as ours, consistently orthodox Catholics will constitute a minority within their religious community" (14). Still, he concluded that "orthodoxy rather than accommodationism [to progressive ideas and behavior] offers greater promise for the future" of the Church (16).

Claimed authority also varies in scope. A teacher may claim a wide or a narrow domain. Similarly, the follower has conceptions of how broad the leader's authority really is. This is the source of the frequently heard statement "I wish those priests would stay out of politics and stick to religious things they know something about." In turn, followers may make claims for their own authority when they find official authority threatening their own beliefs. For example, we are currently witnessing a strong move by conservative believers, both Protestant and Catholic, to challenge the public schools' academic courses on biological evolution. These people are not only challenging the claimed authority of the teachers of biology but also making a claim of their own for what they have called "creation science" or, more recently, "intelligent design." They use the mechanisms of a democratic society (media, public pressure on teachers, and school officials) to achieve their goals.

An obvious case of the breakdown in accepted authority among Catholics is that the vast majority of Catholic couples use some form of birth control, which *Humanae Vitae* disallows, and the great majority do not see their behavior as sinful. Research has monitored the change in Catholic attitudes and behavior in this regard. In 1963, over half of American Catholics accepted the Church's teaching that contraceptive birth control was wrong; in a 1987 poll, only 18 percent said it was wrong (*Los Angeles Times* 1987). A 1993 survey found only 13 percent of Catholics holding that conviction. In that survey, only 12 percent of Catholics under age fifty said that they agreed with "all" Church teaching on faith and morality; of those fifty and older, the figure was 28 percent (*USA Today* 1993). The act of disobeying or simply ignoring a Church pronouncement, especially when a person knows that millions of others are also doing it, creates alienation from the pronouncement itself.[3]

Further evidence that the authority of the Vatican was seriously weakened during the middle period of the twentieth century is found in a series of polls asking American Catholics to agree or disagree with this statement: "Jesus directly handed over the leadership of His Church to Peter and the popes." In 1963, 86 percent agreed the statement was certainly or probably true; in 1974, 71 percent agreed; and in 1985, 68 percent agreed (Hoge 1987, 57), a decline of eighteen points in a span of twenty-two years. Part of the change may be related to the acceptance of the right to freedom of conscience for all Catholics, written into the documents of Vatican II. Catholics increasingly look to their own informed consciences in deciding what they will believe, even on such fundamental teachings as the Petrine principle of Church authority.

Other events besides Vatican II caused change. The political and cultural turmoil in the United Sates in the 1960s undoubtedly had an effect. The powerful experiences of those years heightened mistrust of all institutions among many Americans, especially the young. When the dissembling of national leaders and even presidents was revealed during the Vietnam era, when the duplicity of President Nixon came to light in the Watergate scandal, and when a president and other beloved national figures were assassinated, skepticism about government rose to new heights. Many people concluded that the whole system was rotten. They lost faith in government, and that faith has never returned to its pre-1970 level.

Finally, there is the split that occurred within the hierarchy of the American Church in the 1980s. Following the public presentation of the Peace Pastoral in 1983, Cardinal Joseph Bernardin gave a series of public lectures in December 1983 and early 1984 in which he proposed that the Catholic Church leaders open a national dialogue in the public arena on what he called a "Consistent Ethic of Life." This ethic would focus on life from conception to death. He believed that the Church's teachings were strong enough to sustain a national dialogue. Conservative Catholics, led by Cardinal Bernard Law of Boston, disagreed and insisted that the part of any dialogue dealing with conception was not open to discussion, saying that the Church's position in opposition to abortion under any circumstances precluded including the prebirth period in the moral dialogue. Shortly thereafter, conservative Catholics, including bishops, began to criticize Catholic political leaders such as Governor Mario Cuomo of New York and Democratic vice-presidential candidate Geraldine Ferraro, who said that they were personally opposed to abortion but did not believe that they should impose their beliefs on others in a pluralistic society. Since 1984, this issue has been at the center of the split among Catholics in the political and religious circles. For one group of Catholics, abortion is the litmus test for Catholic orthodoxy; for another group, it has become the focal point for the primacy of conscience.

TEACHING AUTHORITY AND THE GROWING DIVIDE: KEY FINDINGS

To assess accepted authority by Catholic laity, we used two sets of survey questions. The first was introduced in chapter 2 (see figure 2.1) and asked

---

3. The degree to which the teaching against contraception is ignored was acknowledged by Father John McCloskey (2006) in his newsletter to his predominantly conservative readers: "Unfortunately, but not surprisingly, Catholics tend to contracept at the same rate as the rest of the world." He went on to suggest that "one of the major issues for the Church in the decades ahead will be clarity as to who is considered a practicing Catholic and who is not. This may result in a smaller but much more fervent and evangelizing Church" (11).

how important various elements of being a Catholic are felt to be. Table 6.1 includes the four elements of the series of twelve that the respondents rated as most important. It provides evidence that in some areas of teachings there is a high level of acceptance. Three out of four Catholics in the 2005 survey said that the four teachings in table 6.1 were very important to them. All four are rooted deep in Catholic Church history, and we may say that they are accepted as basic or core elements of their faith. Even the youngest generation of Catholics, the Millennials, accept these teachings. Hispanics agree with European Catholics. The findings show that the women were slightly more accepting of these beliefs than were the men and that only with regard to the teaching of Mary as the Mother of God were the Millennials significantly less accepting than the older generations. Although these teachings have deep roots, it is important that Pope John Paul II spoke out often about the importance of these core elements. These teachings had the same high level of acceptance in the 1999 survey. We have no comparable data prior to 1999.

Table 6.2 presents a different picture. It contains the four teachings that lay Catholics considered least important of the series of twelve. Only four in ten Catholics said the Church's teaching in opposition to abortion was very important to them. In addition, only one in three said the teaching in opposition to the death penalty was very important, and only 29 percent

Table 6.1. Catholics Who Say Specific Church Teachings Are Very Important to Them, by Gender, Ethnicity, and Generation, 2005 (in percentages)

	Helping the poor %	Belief in Jesus' resurrection %	Sacraments %	Mary as Mother of God %
Total	84	84	76	74
Gender				
Men	77	81	72	69
Women	91	86	79	78
Ethnicity				
Hispanic	88	80	75	72
Non-Hispanic	84	85	76	74
Generation				
Pre–Vatican II	84	85	82	79
Vatican II	82	83	75	77
Post–Vatican II	84	85	74	71
Millennial	91	81	77	61

Table 6.2. Four Teachings Receiving the Least Acceptance by Catholics as Being Very Important to Them, by Gender, Ethnicity, and Generation, 2005 (in percentages)

	Percentages saying very important to them			
	Teachings that oppose abortion %	Teaching authority claimed by the Vatican %	Teachings that oppose death penalty %	A celibate male clergy %
Total	44	42	35	29
Gender				
Men	46	45	33	30
Women	42	39	37	28
Ethnicity				
Hispanic	40	51	41	32
Non-Hispanic	44	40	35	29
Generation				
Pre–Vatican II	58	52	38	36
Vatican II	44	40	34	25
Post–Vatican II	45	42	34	35
Millennial	7	27	39	11

said a celibate male clergy was very important. Lay Catholics did not see these teachings as important or central, even though Pope John Paul II taught them constantly. He was an outspoken opponent of abortion throughout his twenty-seven-year reign. In his later years, he also spoke out against the death penalty, made special pleas to American Catholics and U.S. governors to spare the lives of particular death penalty inmates, and even forgave the person who tried to assassinate him. He proclaimed the importance of the Church's teaching role and defended the "gift" of the celibate clergy.

There were no gender differences on the latter teachings; men and women generally agreed. On only one item were Hispanics different from European Catholics, half the Hispanics strongly agreeing that the teaching authority of the Vatican was very important to them. The differences were more significant across the generations on three of the four items, revealing a gap between the older and younger age-groups. With the four teachings in table 6.2, we see that Church authority is not accepted on all teachings. Lay Catholics are making choices.

CATHOLICS AND THE LOCUS OF MORAL
AUTHORITY ON ISSUES RELATING
TO HUMAN SEXUALITY

We also asked a series of questions about who should have the final say about issues involving sexual morality. We focused on five teachings that were the subject of ongoing discussion during the papacy of John Paul II and that have also been on the agenda in local and national politics: divorce and remarriage without a Church annulment, contraceptive birth control, abortion, homosexual behavior, and nonmarital sexual relations. Throughout his world travels, John Paul II spoke loudly and consistently in condemnation of the five. Our surveys allow us to see how much authority American Catholics accord to Church leaders regarding these teachings. The following question was asked in 1987, 1993, 1999, and 2005:

> I would like your opinion on several issues that involve moral authority in the Catholic Church. In each case I would like to know who you think should have the final say about what is right or wrong. Is it the Church leaders such as the pope and the bishops, or individuals taking Church teachings into account and deciding for themselves, or both individuals and leaders working together?

Table 6.3 presents the overall trends on each of the five teachings, comparing the averages for Church leaders, individuals, and for both. In 1987, about one in three Catholics saw Church leaders as the proper source of authority on the teachings of abortion, homosexual behavior, and nonmarital sex. By 2005, the percentages for Church leaders on these teachings had declined to one in four. The percentages in 1987 looking to Church leaders on divorce and remarriage (23 percent) and on birth control (12 percent) remained steady over time. The topic on which the 2005 respondents saw the least Church authority was birth control; less than one in seven Catholics in 2005 saw Church leaders as the locus of authority in that regard.

Regarding contraception, support for individual conscience was highest (of the five teachings) in 1987, and it remained steady at 61 percent in 2005. In respondents' choice of "individuals," the only significant change over time occurred on one teaching—divorce and remarriage, which had an 11-percentage-point increase toward individual moral authority.

Perhaps the most interesting finding was the number of respondents who said "both" (see bottom of table 6.3). Large numbers of Catholics want dialogue between individuals and Church leaders.[4] On three of the five teachings (abortion, homosexual behavior, and nonmarital sex), the respondents increased their preference for dialogue. In these three cases, the

Table 6.3.   Catholics Who Look to Church Leaders, Individuals, or Both as the Proper Locus of Moral Authority on Five Teachings Regarding Human Sexuality, 1987–2005 (in percentages)

	1987 %	1993 %	1999 %	2005 %
Church leaders				
Divorce and remarriage without an annulment	23	23	19	22
Practicing contraceptive birth control	12	14	10	13
Advocating choice regarding abortion	29	21	20	25
Engaging in homosexual behavior	32	26	20	24
Engaging in nonmarital sex	34	23	23	22
Individuals (themselves)				
Divorce and remarriage without an annulment	31	38	45	42
Practicing contraceptive birth control	62	57	62	61
Advocating choice regarding abortion	45	44	47	44
Engaging in homosexual behavior	39	39	49	46
Engaging in nonmarital sex	42	44	47	47
Both				
Divorce and remarriage without an annulment	43	37	32	35
Practicing contraceptive birth control	23	26	23	27
Advocating choice regarding abortion	22	33	29	30
Engaging in homosexual behavior	19	30	25	28
Engaging in nonmarital sex	21	30	26	30

increases came at the expense of moral authority of Church leaders alone. By 2005, there was more support for both laity and Church leaders working together than for looking to Church leaders alone.

Most notable is that the highest percentage of votes for laypeople and Church leaders working together occurred over the teaching on divorce and remarriage without an annulment. Perhaps this change reflects the fact that in the past forty years, many Catholics have experienced divorces among family and friends, leading them to more sympathetic attitudes and thus to the desire for a reconsideration of the Church's traditional teaching on divorce. It may also be a reflection of the increased participation of lay professionals in diocesan tribunals involving annulments.

In the next section, we look at specific groups of laity using data from

---

4. When we first formulated this question in 1987, we offered only two options: Church leaders or individuals. During the pretest period, many respondents said they would prefer a third option, namely, a dialogue between Church leaders and Catholic laity. We added it as a third option and subsequently found that it gained support over time.

1987 and 2005. The trend lines from 1987 to 2005 are constant, so there is no need to include the findings from 1993 and 1999 in the tables. In addition, we focus most of our attention on the acceptance of Church leaders as the locus of moral authority because their acceptance rates are the ones that suffered the most decline.

GENDER AND MORAL AUTHORITY

Figure 6.1 compares Catholic men's and women's responses to questions about teaching about gender and moral authority. In 1987, there were no significant differences in their responses. Overall, between one in three and one in four Catholic men and women, respectively, continued to see

1987

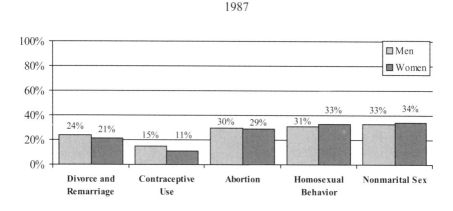

2005

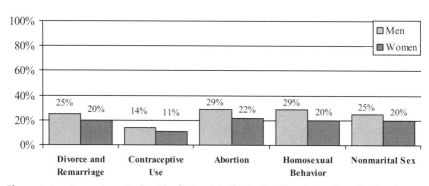

Figure 6.1. Percentage Seeing Final Moral Authority in Church Leaders, by Gender

Church leaders as the locus of moral authority on these teachings. For the men, the findings remained stable over time except for a decline in support for the teaching on nonmarital sex. The women decreased in their acceptance of Church leaders as the proper locus of authority for the teachings on abortion (down 7 percentage points), homosexual behavior (down 13 percentage points), and nonmarital sex (down 14 percentage points).

By 2005, the differences between the men and women in terms of seeing the individual as the proper locus of moral authority had become significant on four of the five teachings: divorce and remarriage: 38 percent of men versus 45 percent of women; contraception: 55 percent versus 66 percent; abortion: 39 percent versus 49 percent; homosexual behavior: 39 percent versus 51 percent; and nonmarital sex: 41 percent versus 51 percent. Thus, over time, women looked more to themselves and less to Church leaders than did men (the data are not shown in figure 6.1).

MORAL AUTHORITY ACROSS GENERATIONS

In 1987, we compared the three generations of Catholics and found that pre–Vatican II Catholics were most accepting of the claims of Church leaders on all five of the teachings, with Vatican II Catholics in the middle and post–Vatican II Catholics least accepting. The three teachings receiving the widest acceptance of Church leaders by all three generations were nonmarital sex, homosexual behavior, and the opposition to abortion.

In 2005, pre–Vatican II Catholics were still the most likely to accept Church leaders' claims; nevertheless, on four of the five teachings, their support had declined significantly (see figure 6.2). Whereas in 1987 more than four in ten senior Catholics accepted the claims of Church leaders on abortion, homosexual behavior, and nonmarital sex, their acceptance level had dropped to three in ten by 2005. Among Vatican II Catholics, the acceptance rates remained more stable, ranging from a low of 11 percent (contraception) to 32 percent (homosexual behavior) in 1987 and declining significantly only with regard to nonmarital sex. Post–Vatican II Catholics also were basically stable from 1987 to 2005 in their acceptance of Church authority. The Millennials, making up only a small portion (9 percent) of the total sample in 2005, need close watching in coming years, given their limited number in our survey. In summary, there was a decline in acceptance of Church leaders within and across generations, with the long-term trends pointing toward further declines.

Catholics have increasingly seen authority in individual consciences. As the acceptance of Church leaders as the locus of moral authority declines, individual authority increases (see figure 6.3). There were increases between 1987 and 2005 regarding divorce and remarriage and homosexual behav-

1987

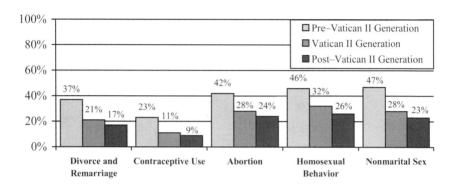

2005

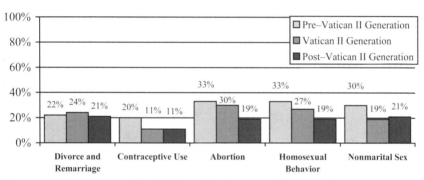

Figure 6.2. Percentage Seeing Final Moral Authority in Church Leaders, by Generation

ior. The largest increase occurred among pre–Vatican II Catholics on their attitudes toward homosexual behavior and nonmarital sex. Vatican II Catholics turned to individual conscience on divorce and remarriage (up 16 points). Post–Vatican II Catholics changed little during the eighteen years.

The bishops have declared abortion to be the most important moral issue facing Catholics. Figure 6.4 depicts the differences in responses regarding the teaching on abortion for the pre–Vatican II and the post–Vatican II generations. The top two circles show that acceptance of Church leaders as the proper locus of moral authority declined by 9 percentage points, acceptance of individuals declined by 3 percentage points, and laity and Church leaders working together increased by 17 percentage points. Among the young generation of Catholics, acceptance of Church leaders

1987

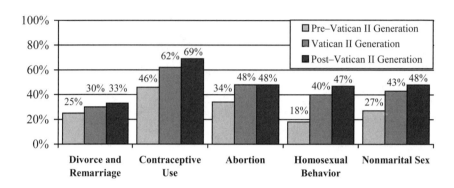

2005

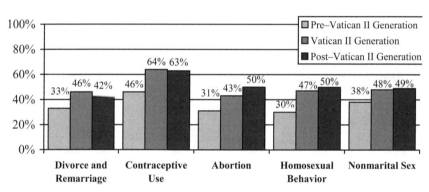

Figure 6.3. Percentage Seeing Final Moral Authority in Individuals, by Generation

declined by 5 points, individuals increased by 2 points to 50 percent, and both working together increased by 5 points to 31 percent. Thus, we find that three out of ten of the oldest and youngest generation would like to see laity working with Church leaders as the proper locus of moral authority. Similar findings resulted when we examined the responses of the high-commitment Catholics; an average of one in three said they would like to see leaders and laity working together. These results are at variance with Church leaders who state that these teachings are anchored in natural law and not subject to discussion of any sort.

In summary, acceptance of the Church's teaching authority on these moral issues has declined across all generations of adult Catholics as laypersons increasingly look to themselves. At the same time, a growing

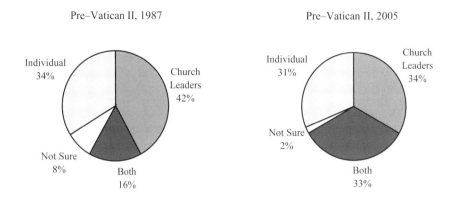

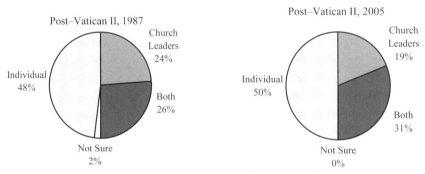

Figure 6.4. Percentage Seeing Final Authority on Choice Regarding Abortion, by Generation, 1987 and 2005 (the post–Vatican II generation includes Millennials in 2005)

minority of Catholics, including the highly committed, would like to see moral-authority teachings resting with both Church leaders and individuals in some kind of dialogue. We will return to this finding in the concluding section.

A YOUNG ADULT TALKS
ABOUT MORAL AUTHORITY

Our interviews demonstrated how many young adult Catholics think about moral authority. Here, as an example, is an educated Catholic woman, age thirty-three, of Polish ethnicity, whom we will call Kate. She grew up in

Ohio, works as a lawyer, and was married three years ago. She exemplifies the complexities of many young persons' views, especially on moral questions.

Interviewer: Do you think it is almost always wrong, or not, to use condoms or birth control pills to prevent pregnancy?

Kate: No, it is not always wrong. It's not always wrong because the consequences of unprotected sex can be ones that aren't desired. And I don't think it's wrong to have sex for pleasure. And it's certainly not wrong to use a condom when you're talking about nonconsensual sex. I don't think birth control is wrong. I just got married, so I'm thinking in terms of a couple making decisions, though I know it's not always in that situation—but, I think for a couple, it's okay to use birth control pills or condoms when they decide they don't want to risk pregnancy. I think it's very responsible to not bring a life into this world if you're not going to take care of it.

Interviewer: Maybe it depends on the circumstances.

Kate: There are certain circumstances when it would be wrong to use birth control pills. Suppose you have a couple where the man is desirous to have children and the woman isn't, and she's using birth control without his knowledge. It would be dishonest. But that's an honesty question rather than whether those things are intrinsically wrong.

Interviewer: That raises another question. If the Church says it's wrong, and you think it's not wrong, maybe that reflects back on the Church's teachings.

Kate: Yes, I think the Church has that wrong.

Interviewer: So that raises another question. Maybe some of the other things it says are wrong too.

Kate: Yes, I think the Church is wrong in a lot of the areas about sex. Even in the mainstream media you hear what's coming out of the Vatican. I understand that these issues are not ones that they are going to budge on right now, especially premarital sex. The sex-outside-of-marriage issue is one that challenges a lot of young people in this country, and it's one that is forming a wedge between young people and the Church.

Interviewer: Here is another question. Do you think that it is always morally wrong to terminate a pregnancy by having an abortion?

Kate: No.

Interviewer: Would there be certain circumstances that would affect that?

Kate: Well, number one, I think any abortion at all would be a sad thing. No matter what. I don't think abortion should be thought of as a birth control method. I think it should be a last resort in limited cases, in cases of rape or incest or endangering the mother's life. I saw an interesting sign on the subway. It said something like "Abortion is a reflection that society has not yet let women have their rights." That spoke to me. This issue bothers me personally. I know where the Church stands on it, and I don't have any beefs with the Church about it. But where it bugs me is that, like I said, I think abortion should be a last resort, and I would hope it would happen as infrequently as possible. But at the same time, I don't want anybody trying to restrict women's rights to have it done.

Interviewer: Do you think it is always morally wrong, or not, to engage in homosexual acts?

Kate: I don't think it is. I just don't. I can't articulate why, I guess. It's like I'm kind of somewhat libertarian, like, I don't have much to say about what other people do, unless someone is harming one another or doing something against their will. If it's their business, it's their business. It's nice that some of the people find somebody to love in this short life. If people want to express themselves homosexually, be physical, and there's no love there, I suppose I don't have a problem with that either. I don't really like to say too much about what goes on in other people's bedrooms. It's just not my thing.

[Kate accepts Church authority in many other matters.]

Interviewer: Some people say that lay people should participate in selecting their parish priests. Do you agree with that, or not?

Kate: No. I don't. Because it's not supposed to be a popularity contest. It's not a priority for me that laity have some say in selecting their priest.

Interviewer: Some people think that lay people should have a right to participate in deciding how parish income should be spent. What do you think?

Kate: I don't think they should have a role in that. It should be up to the priest, on the theory that he's taking orders from somewhere else.

Interviewer: That is, you trust the system.

Kate: I think I do.

DISCUSSION AND CONCLUSION

This chapter has focused on the teaching authority claimed by the Catholic Church. We reviewed the nature of the Church's claims to authority over time and pointed out that during the course of our four surveys, 1987 to 2005, Pope John Paul II was a strong and firm advocate for the Church's teaching authority. He carried his message to all corners of the earth. Whether it was encouraging Catholics to attend Mass more frequently, reclaiming the sacrament of reconciliation, or calling young people to personal lives of holiness and greater commitment to social justice, his voice was strong. He won widespread acclaim as the dominant religious leader of the last quarter of the twentieth century. Our surveys, which were done during two-thirds of his pontificate, provide a measure of the degree to which the Church's teachings on these moral issues continue to be accepted by the laity.

There is continued high acceptance of the Church's teachings on helping the poor, belief in Jesus' resurrection, the sacraments, and in Mary as the Mother of God. However, support declined on issues like abortion, opposition to the death penalty, and a celibate male clergy. Over time, Catholics moved away from looking to Church leaders as the appropriate source of moral authority and toward the individual. At the same time, a minority of

Catholics (about 30 percent) stated that the appropriate source of authority should be both laity and Church leaders working together. By 2005, more Catholics selected this option as the proper source of authority than they selected Church leaders. We explore the implications of this trend in the concluding chapter.

7

Church Leadership and Lay Involvement

Our mother and daughter are sitting again in the coffee shop, enjoying a late Sunday afternoon moment together before heading in their separate directions. The mother, who has just learned that her parish's pastor will not be replaced when he retires next fall, is quite worried. "I've heard that the bishop is making plans to close several of the parishes downtown and merge them all into one or two new parishes," she said. "It just won't be the same, I'm afraid, if we all have to squeeze into St. Malachy's for Mass. We can't even walk there, and I hate to take the car out on a Sunday morning. Besides, how is one priest supposed to handle three or four different communities at once?"

"Oh, Mother," sighed the daughter, "You've become so accustomed to having the priests take all the responsibility for parish life that you just can't imagine another way. My friends tell me that the parish in the suburb near me is bursting at the seams, with five Masses each weekend just to hold all the people. They've even begun a special children's liturgy on Sunday mornings in the school gym to make more room for families with small children. It's like a three-ring circus in the parking lot on Sunday mornings, but the priest there has lots of help from lay committees to ensure that everything flows smoothly. The new pastor at St. Malachy's will have to ask the parishioners to work together with him to lead the parish. Any new pastor who thinks he can do it all on his own is in for a wake-up call when he sees what Catholics today expect out of parish life."

This conversation raises questions about how decisions are made in the Church and who is making them. For example, how do laypeople perceive the leaders of their dioceses and parishes, especially in the wake of the sexual abuse scandal? How much and in what ways do laypeople want to be involved in decisions affecting their parishes and dioceses? Have their attitudes about women's roles in the Church changed in recent years and, if so, in what ways? In this chapter, we begin by examining lay peoples' attitudes toward bishops and other Church leaders today, particularly in light of the recent sexual abuse scandal. From there, we focus attention on leadership and decision making at the parish level. Using research from our current and previous studies, we explore the variety of decision-making roles that are available to lay Catholics and their attitudes toward expanding those roles. Finally, we explore lay Catholics' attitudes toward several alternatives for parish leadership in light of the shortage of priests.

ATTITUDES TOWARD CHURCH LEADERSHIP

As far as most lay Catholics are concerned, their church is their local parish. They are not particularly aware of or concerned with bishops and diocesan affairs. When we asked Catholics in our 2003 survey for the name of their bishop, only four in ten could come up with a name (Davidson and Hoge 2004). We also asked Catholics how much they know about the American bishops and their activities. Only about a third said they know "something" or "a great deal" about the bishops. Four in ten said they know "not much," and more than a quarter said "nothing" or "I don't know." We asked those who said they know "not much" or more to respond to five statements about the bishops (see table 7.1). Their ratings of the bishops ranged from slightly positive to quite mixed. Roughly half said that most bishops are "humble men of great faith" and that "they are doing the best they can under difficult circumstances." Four in ten agreed that most bishops "are wise and competent leaders." Only a fourth agreed that most of the bishops were "more interested in protecting bishops and priests than in

Table 7.1. Catholics' Attitudes about U.S. Bishops, 2003 (percentage saying that each statement applies to "most bishops")

	%
They are doing the best they can under difficult circumstances	51
They are humble men of great personal faith	49
They are wise and competent leaders	43
They are more interested in protecting bishops and priests than in working together with lay people	26
They are out of touch with lay people	25

Note: Questions were asked only of those who said they knew something about bishops.

working with laypeople" and that the bishops were "out of touch with lay-people."

The Center for Applied Research in the Apostolate (CARA) has been monitoring satisfaction with Church leadership since 2000 with the question "How satisfied are you with the leadership of the Catholic Church?" The question measures overall satisfaction only in the abstract and does not specify particular Church leaders or areas of leadership. Satisfaction with the leadership of individual bishops or agreement with the leadership of the U.S. bishops on particular issues can often vary widely from this measure of general satisfaction, as we saw in the previous chapter. Poll results on this overall measure of satisfaction have a mild U-shaped pattern (not shown here), suggesting that Catholics' overall satisfaction with Church leadership declined as a result of the sexual abuse scandal and then rebounded to previous levels of satisfaction (Gray and Perl 2006). Beginning in 2002, CARA also monitored satisfaction with "the leadership of the bishops of the United States" and "the leadership of your local bishop or cardinal." Both of these more specific measures of satisfaction declined somewhat from April to May 2002 but returned to even higher levels of satisfaction in later polls (see figure 7.1). It is important to note that at all times, satisfaction with the leadership of the local bishop or cardinal was

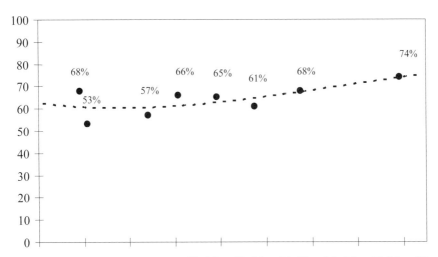

Figure 7.1. How Satisfied Are You with the Leadership of the Bishops of the United States? (percentage "somewhat" or "very" satisfied)

Widespread media coverage of abuse allegations began in February, 2002.
Source: The CARA Polls, April 2002 to October 2005.

higher than with the bishops of the United States taken together (data are not shown here). This is a common pattern in opinion research—people tend to express a higher opinion of their local leadership than they do of more distant higher-level leadership. Nevertheless, by 2005, about three in four Catholics were saying that they are "somewhat" or "very" satisfied with the leadership of the bishops overall.

Lay Involvement in Parish Life

Most Catholics are aware on some level that Catholicism is a global religion, with an elected pope as its head and bishops appointed by him to oversee geographic territories called dioceses, but the parish is where most of them experience the Church. It is the primary place where they participate in the sacramental life of the Church and the primary place where they interact with other Catholics. Accordingly, when lay Catholics are asked about their role in the Church, the question usually brings to their minds activities in the local parish community or in another small Christian community (see Lee and D'Antonio 2000).

The local parish community is increasingly a large, busy place, with activities for all ages and interests and with more opportunity for lay involvement than ever before. In fact, more than a quarter of all U.S. Catholic parishes are of a size equivalent to what would be considered a "megachurch" in Protestant terminology—they have more than 1,200 registered households and more than 3,000 parishioners (Gautier and Perl 2000). These very large parishes typically offer five or more Masses on a weekend to accommodate the large number of parishioners. Often, at least one Mass is offered in a language other than English. In fact, the Archdiocese of Los Angeles reports on its website that it celebrates Masses in more than thirty languages.

Nearly all these outsize "megaparishes" have a resident pastor and usually one associate priest. In addition, they employ an average of four lay ecclesial ministers—laypeople employed at least part time in an administrative or ministerial capacity. These lay Catholics fill a variety of roles that were formerly reserved for priests or women religious, such as pastoral associate, director of religious education, director of adult faith formation, youth minister, and so on. Recent studies have documented that at least 30,000 lay Catholics work in some capacity for the Church at local and diocesan levels (Delambo 2005); another 20,000 or so are enrolled in formation programs around the country (Gautier 2005).

As the numbers of priests and vowed religious continue to decline while the numbers of Catholics continue to increase, lay Catholics are discovering even more opportunities for participation in parish life, some of them involving very close collaboration with clergy. The revised Code of Canon

Law (1983) mandated that every parish have a finance council in which "the Christian faithful . . . aid the pastor in the administration of parish goods" (Canon 537). The Code also recommended, in Canon 536, that "a pastoral council is to be established in each parish; the pastor presides over it, and through it the Christian faithful along with those who share in the pastoral care of the parish . . . give their help in fostering pastoral activity." These and many other opportunities are opening up new avenues for lay involvement in the Church. Such involvement was unimaginable in the immigrant Church of a century ago, in which lay Catholics were expected to "pay, pray, and obey."

Attitudes toward Parish Life Today

Despite the increasing size and complexity of Catholic parishes, most laypeople appear to be comfortable there and to be satisfied with parish life. In 2005, only 40 percent agreed that "Catholic parishes are too big and impersonal," and there was no significant change in this since 1999 (see table 7.2). Further, more than nine in ten Catholics agreed that "on the whole, parish priests do a good job."

However, the two other statements in the table indicate some potentially more disturbing developments over time. Lay Catholics were increasingly likely to agree that "Catholic Church leaders are out of touch with the laity" and that "most priests don't expect the laity to be leaders, just followers." Nearly two-thirds agreed in 2005 that Church leaders are out of touch, compared with just over half in 1999. The younger generations of Catholic laity were more likely than the older generations to agree that Church leaders are out of touch. Among pre–Vatican II and Vatican II Catholics, 60 percent somewhat or strongly agreed that Church leaders are out of touch with the laity, compared with 68 percent of post–Vatican II Catholics. As expected, highly committed Catholics were much *less likely* to somewhat or strongly agree (42 percent), compared with 87 percent of low-commitment Catholics. Even among Catholics who are registered in a parish, 58 percent

Table 7.2.   Attitudes about Church Leaders and Parish Life 1999 and 2005 (percentage responding "somewhat agree" or "strongly agree")

	1999 %	*2005* %
Catholic parishes are too big and impersonal.	46	40
On the whole, parish priests do a good job.	91	91
Catholic church leaders are out of touch with the laity.	53	63
Most priests don't expect the laity to be leaders, just followers.	44	53

somewhat or strongly agreed, compared with 76 percent who are not registered.

Likewise, more than half of Catholic laity (53 percent) agreed in 2005 that priests don't expect the laity to be leaders, compared with 44 percent who agreed with that statement in 1999. These two changes in attitude—that Catholic Church leaders are out of touch with the laity and that priests don't expect the laity to be leaders—signal an evolving understanding among laypeople about their role in the Church. The laity are becoming more assertive as they gain more experience with lay leadership in parishes and dioceses.

In fact, the question about lay leadership has been asked on several previous national surveys of Catholics (see Hoge 1987) and showed a consistent trend on the part of laity in the direction of more support for lay leadership. The percentage of lay Catholics agreeing strongly or somewhat that "most priests don't expect the lay members to be leaders, just followers" was 46 percent in 1963, 44 percent in 1974, and 39 percent in 1985. The percentage in 2005 is not much different from what it was in 1963, suggesting that the increased collaboration among priests and laity that was experienced in the 1970s and 1980s may be declining as the "cultic model" of priesthood gains influence among priests ordained since the 1980s (Hoge and Wenger 2003).

Comparing across generations, 57 percent of pre–Vatican II Catholics agreed somewhat or strongly that "most priests don't expect the laity to be leaders, just followers," compared with 51 percent of Vatican II and 53 percent of post–Vatican II Catholics. These younger Catholics, who have grown up in a Vatican II Church, are accustomed to laypeople in leadership positions in parishes and dioceses, unlike pre–Vatican II Catholics. Nevertheless, more than half still agreed in 2005 that priests don't expect the laity to be leaders. Among Catholics who are registered in a parish, fewer than half (45 percent) agree somewhat or strongly with this statement, compared with 70 percent of Catholics who are not registered. And only 40 percent of highly committed Catholics agree somewhat or strongly, compared to 68 percent of low-commitment Catholics.

Post–Vatican II and Millennial Catholics now constitute half of all adult Catholics in the United States. Two-thirds of them are registered in a parish, and about one in seven are highly committed to the Church. These increasing sentiments that Church leaders are out of touch with the laity and that most priests don't expect laypeople to be leaders could signal increasing friction between lay Catholics and priests in the future.

Findings from other research agree with this possible outcome. Hoge and Wenger (2003, 124ff.) measured trends in attitudes of American priests using repeated surveys over sixteen years and compared them with the trends in lay attitudes described here. The trends are in different directions.

Younger priests today are less and less interested in collaboration with lay leaders in parish life, just the opposite from the trend among laypersons toward greater desire for parish involvement. Hoge and Wenger found that priests today are divided in that groups of priests hold two disparate visions of what a priest essentially is. One vision, which past researchers have called the "cultic model," stresses the sacramental role of priests and the necessity of clear separation from the laity. The other vision, called the "servant-leader model," emphasizes collaborative leadership with the laity, spiritual leadership of the flock, and social leadership in the local community. Prior to the Second Vatican Council, the cultic model was dominant, but after the Council the servant-leader model was widely embraced for a time. Beginning in the 1980s, young priests again preferred the cultic model, which is the one most young priests believe in today. Hence, young priests may be somewhat less collaborative today than in the 1970s and 1980s.

LAY PARTICIPATION IN PARISH DECISIONS

Another aspect of lay involvement in parish life that we have studied over time is lay participation in parish decisions, such as deciding how parish income should be spent or deciding on priests for their parish. Lay Catholics are increasingly supportive of their right to participate in each of these decisions—and is true for all generations, commitment levels, and levels of Catholic identity (see table 7.3). Compared with the levels of agreement we found in 1987, lay Catholics today are more likely to agree that they should have the right to participate in deciding how parish income should be spent (81 percent in 1987; 89 percent in 2005). They are much more likely to agree, too, that they should have the right to participate in selecting priests for their parish (57 percent in 1987; 71 percent in 2005). Two new questions in the 2005 survey add weight to the assertion that the laity are prepared to accept more active participation in parish life: more than eight in

Table 7.3.   Should Catholic Laity Have or Not Have the Right to Participate in . . . ? 1987–2005 (percentage saying "should")

	1987 %	1993 %	1999 %	2005 %
Deciding how parish income should be spent	81	83	86	89
Deciding how diocesan income should be spent	—	—	—	84
Deciding about parish closings	—	—	—	80
Selecting the priests for their parish	57	74	73	71

ten agreed that laity should have the right to participate in diocesan-level decisions, such as spending priorities and parish closings.

Some bishops who have unilaterally imposed parish closings without consulting with the parishioners have reaped opposition from the laity. Today, several dioceses are trying a variety of methods to include parishioners more in this decision-making process. For example, in a study conducted in 2001, CARA found that 72 percent of dioceses had undertaken some sort of parish restructuring between 1995 and 2000 and that about three in four dioceses that had restructured their parishes reportedly had involved parishioners in the decision-making process (Rexhausen et al. 2004). More recently, in the case of the Archdiocese of Boston, when the laity in several parishes felt that they had not been given a fair hearing in regard to the closing of their parishes, they protested in an organized way, and the archbishop modified his plans. This suggests that the laity find the closing of their parishes a salient issue, one on which they want to be heard.

Although the laity are beginning to have their concerns heard on matters of parish closing, decisions about priest assignments continue to be reserved for the bishop, who often consults with the vicar for clergy but seldom solicits input from parishioners. And decisions about parish spending priorities are still reserved for the parish pastor, although he increasingly seeks the advice of a parish finance council or even the parish pastoral council.

On the 2005 survey, we asked Catholics for the first time about whether the laity should have the right to participate in deciding how diocesan income should be spent. We do not have trend data from previous surveys on this opinion, but 84 percent of Catholics in this poll agreed that the laity should have the right to participate in diocesan spending decisions. This agreement holds across generations, income levels, gender, ethnicity, and even level of commitment to the Church. Despite a relatively strong consensus that Church leaders are handling Church finances properly, lay Catholics still think they should have the right to participate in diocesan spending decisions.

In 2003, along with questions about the sexual abuse crisis, we asked questions about Church finances more generally (see table 7.4). More than eight in ten Catholics want financial reports that show how much money has been spent on settling lawsuits against Church leaders, and they agree that the Church needs better financial reporting at all levels. On the question of whether the laity should withhold donations to the Church until they have more voice in financial decisions, however, the majority said no. Most Catholics do not favor challenging the Church in this way.

Evidence from CARA polls also suggests that Catholics still have confidence in the financial abilities of Church leaders, despite the former's desire

Table 7.4.   Financial Decision Making in the Church, 2003 (percentage responding "strongly agree" or "somewhat agree")

	%
Church financial reports should show how much money has been spent on settling lawsuits against Church leaders.	81
The Catholic Church needs better financial reporting at all levels.	77
Catholic lay people should withhold donations to the Church until they have more voice in financial decisions.	40

for more accountability. When asked, "How much confidence, if any, do you have that your bishop or cardinal is properly handling Church finances?" more than three-quarters say they have at least some confidence in his handling of Church finances. Nearly four in ten express "a great deal" of confidence (see table 7.5). Nevertheless, contributions to diocesan financial appeals declined between 2002 and 2005 (Gray and Perl 2006). In a series of surveys conducted between 2002 and 2005 by Charles Zech for Foundations and Donors Interested in Catholic Activities, Inc. (FAD-ICA), approximately one in seven regular Mass attenders—those who are most likely to contribute to parish and diocesan collections—responded that they gave less to diocesan collections, most of them citing anger over the sexual abuse scandal or lack of accountability in diocesan finances as the primary reason (FADICA 2005). Table 7.5 demonstrates that people express greater confidence in the financial accountability of their local leader than they do in the more distant diocesan leadership. The 2005 CARA poll asked laypersons how much confidence they have in the handling of Church finances by 1) their bishop or cardinal and 2) their local pastor. Again, we see that Catholics trust their own local priest, whom they know, more than the bishops or cardinals, who are far away from their parish experience of Church.

Table 7.5.   "How much confidence, if any, do you have that . . ."

	A Great Deal %	Some %	Only a Little %	None %
Your bishop or cardinal is properly handling Church finances?	38	39	16	6
The pastor of your local parish is properly handling Church finances?	54	30	12	4

Source: CARA telephone poll, fall 2005.

The Laity's Changing Role in Parish Finances

In 2005, we also asked Catholics to tell us what best describes the appropriate role for parishioners with respect to parish finances. (The results are shown in figure 7.2.) About two out of three said that parishioners should have input into determining the budget, with the priest having the final say. One in five said that parishioners should have general oversight, with the priest alone responsible for parish finances but reporting to parishioners. Another 14 percent said that parishioners should have the final say over all aspects of parish finances—after all, the money does come from the parishioners themselves. Some 3 percent were at the other end of the spectrum, saying that parishioners should have no role in parish finances and that all parish financial decisions should be made independently by the priest.

In sum, the level of input in parish finances that parishioners are seeking is modest. Most want some input in major financial decisions but trust the pastor to make those decisions for the good of the parish. Only one in seven believes that parishioners should have the final say in financial decisions. Nevertheless, this is an important area of parish life in which Catholics increasingly feel they should play a role. Catholics agree widely on this. Highly committed Catholics express the same attitudes as low-commitment Catholics about parishioners' role in parish finances. Registered parishioners feel the same way as Catholics not registered in a parish, regular Mass attenders are no different from infrequent attenders, and men and women

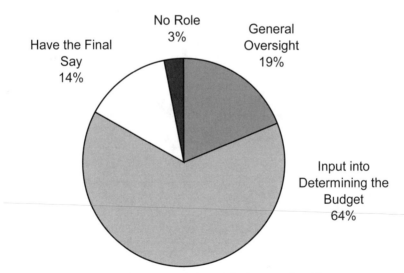

Figure 7.2.   Catholic Parishioners' Role in Parish Finances Should Be . . . (2005)

are in agreement on this issue, as are Catholics in all generations. Hispanics, as well, express similar opinions about their role in parish financial decisions.

Decisions about Parish Life in Light of the Priest Shortage

Financial decisions are not the only area in which Catholics increasingly feel they should have a role. They also have strong opinions about the role of laypeople in other parish decisions. As laid out in table 7.3, more than seven in ten agreed that Catholic laity should have the right to participate in selecting the priests for their parish, and even more feel that they should have the right to participate in deciding about parish closings. Catholics care about possible decisions that could affect their parish life as they hear about parishes being closed in other places and as they gradually become more aware of the priest shortage. As early as 1999, CARA research showed that although almost three-quarters of Catholics had heard of a priest shortage, fewer than a quarter said they had been affected by it (Froehle and Gautier 2000). But in 1999, the priest shortage was less severe—just over half the dioceses in the United States had fewer diocesan priests than parishes. In the intervening six years, the number of parishes declined by 2 percent, but the number of active diocesan priests declined by 11 percent. Laypeople are expressing some definite preferences about parish life, as the numbers of priests available for parish ministry continues to decline.

Our 2005 survey contained a list of changes that some dioceses are making in light of the priest shortage. We asked the laity to tell us how acceptable they would find each change if it were to occur in their parish (see table 7.6). Catholics are willing to accept many alternatives to forestall the likelihood of their parish's being closed. However, each change involves sacrificing some aspect of parish life as they know it, and no alternative was deemed "very acceptable" by a majority of Catholics.

Sharing a priest with one or more other parishes was the most acceptable alternative, deemed at least somewhat acceptable by more than nine in ten laypersons. Catholics of all generations supported this alternative, as did Catholics of all levels of commitment.

In fact, sharing a priest is already a reality in at least a third of all U.S. parishes (Gray and Gautier 2004) and likely to become even more common as bishops restructure parish life to cope with the reality of fewer priests. However, sharing a priest implies much more than merely rearranging the Mass schedule so that the priest from St. Anselm's can get over to St. Anne's in time for the 10:30 liturgy. Parishioners are often called on to play a much larger role in parishes that share a priest; the parishes are often called "linked," "twinned," "paired," "clustered," or "yoked" (see Rexhausen et al. 2004). Many of the parishes with a shared priest also share

Table 7.6. Catholics Willing to Accept This in Their Parish, 2005

	"Somewhat" or "Very" Acceptable %	*"Very" Acceptable* %
Sharing a priest with one or more other parishes	92	39
Bringing in a priest from another country to lead the parish	89	43
Merging two or more nearby parishes into one parish	88	36
Having a Communion service instead of a Mass some of the time	60	12
Not having a resident priest in the parish but only a lay parish administrator and visiting priests	54	10
Reducing the number of Masses to fewer than once a week	40	8
Not having a priest available for visiting the sick	37	5
Closing the parish	30	4
Not having a priest available for administering last rites for the dying	20	5

staff (such as a director of religious education who oversees catechetical ministry in the linked parishes), share programs (such as a combined youth ministry program), and may share committees or organizations (such as a combined liturgy committee). In fact, some clustered parishes each have their own parish pastoral council and together also have a cluster pastoral council. It is no great surprise, then, that priests who pastor multiple parishes say that their workload increased with the addition of another parish. To make the whole complex operation work, priests are increasingly relying on trusted parishioners to take on more of the load and to make decisions for the good of the parish.

Bringing in a priest from another country to lead the parish is another option that nearly nine in ten Catholics say they would find at least "somewhat acceptable." About 85 percent of pre–Vatican II and Vatican II Catholics support such a measure, as do more than 90 percent of post–Vatican II and Millennials. Moreover, highly committed Catholics are just as likely as low-commitment Catholics to say that it would be "very acceptable" to bring in a priest from another country to lead the parish. This option appears quite attractive in the abstract—the diocese is relieved of the pressure to close more parishes, and the parish has a replacement with all the sacramental faculties of the priest it lost. Nevertheless, anecdotal evidence from a number of dioceses suggests that although Catholics might consider this an attractive alternative in the abstract, many parishioners have a very hard time adjusting to a priest from another country (Hoge and Okure 2006). The Church is global, but priests are not interchangeable parts that can easily be substituted one for another. Language differences, cultural differences, and ecclesiological differences sometimes result in an intolerable situation for parishioners and for the priest from another country who is assigned to serve them.

A third alternative that nearly as many Catholics would find at least "somewhat acceptable" is the merging of two or more nearby parishes into one parish. Lay Catholics were about as accepting of this alternative as they were of sharing a priest (88 percent said that mergers are acceptable, and 92 percent said that sharing a priest is acceptable). Catholics of all generations were about equal in their support of this model. However, highly committed Catholics were less likely than low-commitment Catholics (23 percent compared with 46 percent) to say they would find merging parishes at least somewhat acceptable.

This alternative can look, from the outside, very much like a "cluster" model, with one priest visiting multiple parishes to celebrate Mass. But they are different canonically, and the implications for parishioners are substantially different. In the case of a merger of two or more parishes, the parishes involved are technically "suppressed" (Canon Law terminology for closing a parish), and a new parish is created that includes all the territory and people of the suppressed parishes. In other words, even though there still may be two or more church buildings that continue to serve as worship sites, there is only one parish community, composed of all the people who made up the parishes before they were merged. The role of parishioners from the previously separate congregations has to be redefined and renegotiated in light of the new parish structure. This process can become quite contentious, particularly if the parishioners from one parish feel they are being absorbed or subsumed into another parish. In a merger, often one or more church buildings are closed and sometimes sold, two (or more) existing parish staffs must be combined into one, duplicate or multiple parish programs must be coordinated or reconfigured, and previously discrete parish resources must be combined in a fair manner. In the process, parishioners who may have served in a decision-making role before the merger are sometimes left feeling marginalized or left out of important decisions.

Other alternatives for dealing with a shortage of priests that more than half of lay Catholics said would be at least "somewhat acceptable" in their parish included having a Communion service instead of a Mass some of the time and having a lay parish administrator instead of a resident priest. These are both somewhat more drastic measures, and only about 10 percent of Catholics would find either one "very acceptable." Each alternative reduces the ready access to Eucharist, to which U.S. Catholics have become accustomed. Six in ten Catholics said that having a Communion service instead of a Mass some of the time would be at least "somewhat acceptable," although nearly four in ten said this arrangement would be "not at all" acceptable. In a Communion service, a deacon or a layperson leads the congregation in a liturgical service that is structured similar to a Mass. However, instead of the Eucharistic prayer and consecration, previously consecrated and reserved Communion bread is distributed to the congregation. When this Communion service takes the place of a Sunday Mass, it is called Sunday Celebration in the Absence of a Priest. Highly committed Catholics were the most likely to say that a Communion service instead of a Mass would *not be acceptable* at all—54 percent, compared with 27 percent of low-commitment Catholics. Millennial Catholics were less likely than older Catholics to find a Communion service unacceptable. Only 14 percent of Millennial Catholics, compared with 47 percent of post–Vatican II Catholics, 37 percent of Vatican II Catholics, and 40 percent of pre–Vatican II Catholics, said that a Communion service instead of a Mass was not at all acceptable. A growing number of theologians and bishops also worry about potential distortions in Catholics' understanding of the sacrament as the act of consecration becomes separated in peoples' minds from the activity of receiving Communion (see Philibert 2004, 57). Indeed, Catholics themselves seem less open to this alternative today than they were in 1999, when they were somewhat less likely to have experienced it firsthand.

Having a lay parish administrator and visiting priests to celebrate the Mass was acceptable to 54 percent of Catholics. A majority of Catholics of each generation agreed that this alternative would be at least "somewhat acceptable." Again, highly committed Catholics were the *least* likely to accept this alternative (43 percent, compared with 61 percent of low-commitment Catholics). This alternative model for parish leadership was first introduced in the 1983 revised Code of Canon Law, in which Canon 517.2 states,

> If the diocesan bishop should decide that, due to a dearth of priests, participation in the exercise of the pastoral care of a parish is to be entrusted to a deacon or to some other person who is not a priest or to a community of persons. . . .

The United States already has more than 550 parishes that are entrusted to someone other than a priest (Gray and Gautier 2004). A quarter of those parishes are led by a deacon, half are entrusted to a religious sister or brother, and a quarter are entrusted to a layperson. This is virtually uncharted territory in terms of a role for laity, but the response to having a layperson leading a parish has been mostly positive (see Wallace 1992, 2003). In this model, the bishop hires a deacon or a layperson (including religious sisters and brothers) to assume responsibility for the day-to-day administrative and pastoral care of a parish. A priest is also assigned as pastor, but he typically does not reside at the parish and may not even be the sacramental minister (the priest who presides at Mass on Sunday) for the parish. It is most often the responsibility of the lay parish coordinator to secure the services of a priest for Sunday Mass. In some cases, when a priest is not available, the lay parish coordinator may offer a Communion service in place of a Mass. This option is used very sparingly, though, and fewer than one in ten lay parish coordinators say they offer Sunday Celebrations in the Absence of a Priest (Gray and Gautier 2004).

We also have trend data on most of the alternatives for dealing with the shortage of priests, as can be seen in table 7.7. Aside from occasional Communion services and lay parish administrators, none of the other alternatives was even "somewhat" acceptable to a majority of Catholics. In general, the trends since 1987 demonstrate that lay Catholics are more accepting now of the alternatives in table 7.7 than they were in 1987. The largest shift was from 1987 to 1993, with little change since then. Catholics today seem more accepting than they were two decades ago about the possibilities of not having a resident priest in their parish, not having Mass at least once a week, not having a priest available to visit the sick, and not having a priest

Table 7.7. Trends in Acceptance of Parish Leadership Alternatives, 1987–2005 (percentage responding "very acceptable" or "somewhat acceptable")

	1987 %	1993 %	1999 %	2005 %
Sharing a priest with one or more other parishes	—	—	—	92
Bringing in a priest from another country to lead the parish	—	—	—	89
Merging two or more nearby parishes into one parish	—	—	—	88
Having a Communion service instead of a Mass some of the time	—	—	68	60
Not having a resident priest in the parish but only a lay parish administrator and visiting priests	39	56	51	54
Reducing the number of Masses to fewer than once a week	28	41	41	40
Not having a priest available for visiting the sick	24	41	34	37
Closing the parish	—	—	—	30
Not having a priest available for administering last rites for the dying	15	30	20	20

available to administer the last rites. The higher rates of acceptance are partly a result of the attitudes of young Catholics, as described previously.

Leadership Roles for Women

The Church today has an expanding number of leadership roles that are open to women, and laywomen are increasingly present in parish leadership, many of them taking over positions of responsibility that formerly were filled by women religious (Froehle and Gautier 2000, 133). CARA's telephone poll of parish lay ministers documented in 2002 that about 80 percent of parish lay ecclesial ministers are women (Gray and Gautier 2004). The National Pastoral Life Center found the same percentage of women in its 2005 study of parish lay ministers (Delambo 2005). Although the clergy is a leadership role that is still closed to women, there are a number of other positions that are not. Many of the roles that were once the exclusive domain of men are now increasingly occupied by women. In 1999 and 2005, we asked about lay support for women serving in a variety of roles in the Church. We found strong support for women in these roles (see table 7.8); the clear majority of Catholics supported women serving in all six leadership roles.

More than 80 percent of Catholics supported women as altar servers, as Eucharistic ministers, as parish administrators (in parishes that do not have a resident priest pastor), and even as deacons—although the role of deacon is not open to women at this time. Unlike the divergence of opinion regarding support for women priests (reported in chapter 5), we found no significant generational differences in support for women in these other roles. Men and women were equally likely to support these roles for women in the Church. Age, education, Catholic schooling, and income had no influence on support for these roles for women. We did find, however, that commitment to the Church had a moderate influence in the direction of reduced support for women as deacons or as priests. Nevertheless, even

Table 7.8.   Support for Women in Leadership Roles in the Church, 1999 and 2005 (percentage supporting)

	1999 %	2005 %
Altar server	—	93
Lector	86	—
Parish administrator	—	93
Eucharistic minister	83	90
Deacon	77	81
Priest	64	63

among highly committed Catholics, 68 percent expressed support for women deacons, and 40 percent supported women priests.

CONCLUSION

What do these findings mean for the Church? The data suggest that the connection to parish life remains strong among the Catholic laity. As Catholic parishes grow larger and more complex and as the priests available to serve in them continue to age and decline in number, the role of Catholic laity in parish life becomes ever more visible. However, an increased role for laypersons in parish life is sure to come into conflict with the traditional authority and decision-making structures that have defined parish life until today. The more parishioners feel that it is their right and obligation to participate in parish decisions, the greater will be the challenge to pastors to find ways to increase collaboration in decision making.

Most Catholics are relatively satisfied with parish life as it is structured today. They agree that, on the whole, parish priests do a good job. And even though Catholic parishes are becoming increasingly large and complex, most Catholics do not believe that they are too large and impersonal. What lay Catholics are calling for is increased participation in decision making within the parish. The increased sentiments that "Church leaders are out of touch with the laity" and that "most priests don't expect laity to be leaders, just followers" signal that more Catholics today perceive that their desire for participation may not be taken seriously by Church leaders. Priests who adhere firmly to the cultic model of priesthood will increasingly find themselves at odds with parishioners who want a voice in parish decisions. These two trends are in conflict with each other.

The vast majority of lay Catholics think that they should have the right to participate in deciding how parish income should be spent, but most would be satisfied if that participation extended only so far as having some input into determining the parish budget. Most agreed that they should have the right to participate in deciding about parish closings, but they were open to a number of alternatives that preserve parish life while attending to the reality of fewer and older parish priests. Lay Catholics think that they should have the right to participate in selecting priests for their parish, but most would find it acceptable to share a priest with another parish.

In sum, Catholic laypeople are asking for a greater voice in parish decisions. They see the role of the Catholic laity in parish life evolving from the old "pay, pray, and obey" model to one in which lay Catholics are increasingly involved in aspects of parish life that were formerly reserved only for clergy. Essentially, they are asking for the same thing the U.S. Bishops are calling for in their recent document on lay ecclesial ministry:

> Co-Workers in the Vineyard of the Lord expresses our strong desire for the fruitful collaboration of ordained and lay ministers who, in distinct but complementary ways, continue in the church the saving mission of Christ for the world, his vineyard. (United States Conference of Catholic Bishops 2005a, 6)

We are not in a position yet to describe what this "fruitful collaboration of ordained and lay ministers" actually will turn out to be. That subject will likely be a component of our next survey in this series.

8

Religion and Politics among American Catholics

If American Catholics wish to have an influence on the nation and the world, they need to pay attention to politics. For better or worse, moral influence in a democracy requires involvement in the political process.

Over the past three or four decades, the Catholic Church has grown in its national influence. This was seen in the presidential campaign of 2004 and in the unprecedented circumstance that five of the nine Supreme Court justices now active are committed Catholics. Our research team decided to look in more detail at Catholics' political views in the aftermath of the 2004 elections. How do Catholics divide along political party lines? Are Mass attendance and other measures of commitment to the Church related to adherence to different political parties? Is Church commitment related to such issues as abortion, government funding for more health care for the poor, and stiffer enforcement of the death penalty—three of the issues that have brought the Catholic Church and the political parties into close contact?

Catholic bishops and Catholic groups are actively involved in political issues. The bishops and Catholic pro-life groups recently played key roles in opposition to abortion, and the bishops, with the encouragement of Pope John Paul II and groups like Pax Christi, have actively opposed the death penalty. The bishops have a lobbying group; their Government Liaison Office lobbies for a wide range of social issues every year before Congress. In addition, the bishops have established Catholic Conferences in thirty-four states, thereby ensuring that their concerns will be heard at both state and federal levels (Yamane 2005).

In addition to the bishops, a cohort of women religious has established its own lobbying group, NETWORK, and through its publications, highlight the legislation it supports or opposes, explaining how it does or does not comport with Catholic social teachings. A variety of other Catholic groups also lobby, many on issues ranging from pro-life (such as Women for Faith and Family) to pro-choice (such as Catholics for a Free Choice) on abortion; on the death penalty; and on help for the poor. In this chapter, we examine the relationship between political party identification of American Catholics and their values, beliefs, and practices on social and moral issues.

A LOOK BACK

The big picture is that Catholic Democrats continue to outnumber Catholic Republicans; however, the gap between these numbers has narrowed to a few percentage points. Catholic support for the Democratic Party peaked with the election of John F. Kennedy, a Catholic, in 1960, then receded. Kennedy received 80 percent of the Catholic vote; in 1964, Lyndon Johnson received 76 percent. Catholics have since been divided. In the ten presidential elections after Johnson, Catholics voted for the Democratic candidate five times and for the Republican five times. In eight of the ten, the candidate with the majority of the Catholic vote won the election. An exception was the 2000 election, in which Al Gore won the Catholic vote by 2 percentage points but lost the electoral vote to George W. Bush.

The 2004 election and the role of religion in it stand in sharp contrast to the election of 1960. A comparison of the two elections, forty-four years apart, will illustrate some changes in the American Catholic community.

In 1960, John F. Kennedy had certain advantages not available to John F. Kerry in 2004. First and foremost was the fact that the Catholic population then was theologically united. Almost three out of four adult Catholics reported going to Mass weekly. Until the 1950s, most had been working class and poor. They had found the New Deal policies of the Roosevelt and Truman administrations attuned to their needs, and they gave the Democratic Party strong support. The New Deal policies were also influenced by a number of Catholic clergy, such as Monsignor John A. Ryan and George Higgins, who worked hard to link Catholic social teachings to the labor movement and Democratic Party policies. The Democratic Party was an amalgam of religioethnic groups and labor unions, strengthened by urban political networks.

Kennedy faced a special and difficult challenge in 1960. He needed to

---

1. Kennedy won over a significant number of black voters by his phone call to Mrs. Martin Luther King Jr. while the Reverend King was in the Birmingham jail for his act of civil disobedience to the South's Jim Crow laws. As a result of that phone call, King announced that he would vote for Kennedy (*Washington Post* 1960).

find a way to maximize the Catholic, Jewish, and black vote and gain enough of the white Protestant vote to win.[1] To do so, he had to blend progressive policies with political realities, particularly his own identity as a Catholic.

Neither abortion nor homosexuality was an issue causing splits in either the Church or the society in 1960. Nor were there groups calling for a married clergy or even women clergy because the Catholic seminaries were full and the women's movement was still several years off. Even birth control had not yet emerged as an issue that divided Catholics. The archbishop of Boston, Cardinal Cushing, was a friend of the Kennedy family, providing the candidate a level of clerical protection that Kerry was never able to enjoy.

Kennedy saw his task as one of convincing Protestants that he would not be a lackey of the Vatican. He also counted on the fact that the Catholic bishops might grumble but would not lash out at him even though they knew he would not support financial aid to parochial schools, a key Catholic issue at the time. A fortuitous factor was the new pope. Pope John XXIII had been in office only a year, and he had won approval for his pastoral approach and his decision to open the windows of the Church to let in some fresh air. In a subtle way, Kennedy benefited from a pope who was himself open to change.

On international matters, Kennedy was not to be outdone by Nixon in his opposition to communism, and he had oratorical skills that enabled him to court the Catholic vote even as he told large Catholic audiences that they should not vote for him just because he was Catholic. At the same time, he told Protestant audiences that he hoped they would not vote against him just because he was Catholic. Meanwhile, Nixon felt that he could not talk about the religious factor without seeming to be biased against Catholics, so he said nothing. Kennedy won 80 percent of the Catholic vote, a large part of the Jewish and black vote, and just enough of the Protestant vote to win the election by a very narrow margin (White and D'Antonio 2007).

Compare that setting with the 2004 election. American Catholics in 2004 were split on the hot-button issues of abortion and same-sex marriage. They were also affected by a sexual abuse scandal that had badly injured the credibility of some members of the hierarchy. At the same time, a majority of Catholics supported the war in Iraq, a war that Pope John Paul II had strongly opposed. Candidate Kerry had also supported the war, and he seemed unable to mount a critique against the war that would have built on his Vietnam-era repulsion against the earlier war. The Republican Party had already made a thoroughgoing effort to lure the Catholic vote in 1999. More than $2.5 million was spent on that drive, led by a wealthy Philadelphia Catholic and a strong supporting cast. In the 2000 election, Catholics gave 49 percent of their votes to Gore and 47 percent to Bush.

By 2004, with Bush in the White House, the Republican Party committed $10 million to mobilize forces and win the majority of the Catholic vote, including special efforts to win Hispanic Catholics to the Republican side. By contrast, the Democratic effort to win over the Catholic vote was slow, hesitant, and poorly funded (D'Antonio 2005). The Republicans joined their efforts with bishops whose opposition to abortion was so strong that they made public statements indicating that should pro-choice candidate Kerry appear in any of their dioceses, he would not be welcome at the Communion rail. The number of bishops who spoke out directly against Kerry was small, but their voices carried weight in the media and were supported indirectly by words from the Vatican. The bishops in their 2004 meeting voted 183 to 6 to approve a document that said the decision to deny Communion "rests with the individual bishop in accord with the established canonical and pastoral principles." Further, their statement "Catholics in Political Life" called on Catholic politicians and political activists to oppose legal abortion "lest they be guilty of cooperating in evil and in sinning against the common good" (Jones and Feuerherd 2004). Kerry was unable to counter these statements.

Kerry had no hometown bishop to give him media support. Meanwhile, in June 2004, President Bush went to Rome for an official visit with the pope, listened quietly while the pope chastised him for the war in Iraq, assured the pope that he was now in the process of rebuilding Iraq, and ended by receiving the pope's blessing for his strong stand against abortion, stem cell research, and same-sex marriage (*New York Times* 2004). Later that summer, Bush managed another photo opportunity when he appeared at the Knights of Columbus national convention. In contrast, Kerry was not invited to visit the pope, nor was he able to contrive comparable photo-ops. He even seemed to avoid them as indecorous. In effect, Kerry was almost as unable to find his way regarding the religious factor as Nixon had been in 1960. As a result, Bush won 52 percent of the Catholic vote.

Conservative Catholics, including more than a dozen bishops, condemned Kerry and other pro-choice Catholics. They dominated the news and in the process made abortion the main Catholic issue, leaving behind other social teachings regarding help to the poor, raising the minimum wage, and taxation—all issues on which Kerry was much closer to the bishops' positions than was Bush. Just as important, perhaps, were the changes in the demographics. Younger Catholics in 2004 were different from Catholics in 1960; they had grown up with much different experiences in both Church and civil society.

In the aftermath of the election, numerous polls (Carville et al. 2005; Finn 2005; Green et al. 2004; Pew Research Center 2005) tried to determine which issues had been salient to the voters. One often-cited finding was that those voters who went to church services regularly, regardless of specific religious denomination, were more likely than nonregular churchgoers to be conservative on issues like abortion and same-sex marriage and to vote Republican. Our 2005 survey gives us additional information on American Catholics in the aftermath of the heated 2004 election year.

AMERICAN CATHOLICS AND ELECTORAL POLITICS

As American Catholics have moved up the socioeconomic ladder, their party loyalties have shifted. Figure 8.1 shows their changes in party identification from 1952 through 2004. Through most of the past fifty years, Catholics continued to identify themselves more as Democrats than as Republicans. Leege et al. (2002) demonstrated how Republicans used a variety of racial/ethnic, military, and cultural issues both to depress the Catholic Democratic vote and to create significant defections, enabling the GOP to win nine of the fourteen presidential elections between 1952 and 2004.

The Catholic presence in national elections goes well beyond presidential elections. A look at the Catholic presence in the U.S. House and Senate (table 8.1) over time shows the changing numbers of Catholics in those

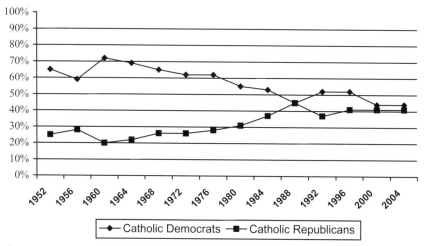

Figure 8.1. White, Non-Latino American Catholics, by Party Identification, 1952–2004

Source: Leege et al. (2002, 161). If Hispanic/Latino Catholics were added, the Democratic figures would be higher. See also Bliss Institute, Akron University, Fourth National Survey of Religion (2004).

Table 8.1. Catholic Members of the U.S. Senate and House of Representatives, by Party, 1976–2004 (actual numbers)

	1976	1980	1984	1988	1992	1996	2000	2004
Catholic senators								
Democratic	12	10	9	13	13	12	14	14
Republican	3	4	9	6	8	9	11	11
Catholic representatives								
Democratic	82	82	88	82	75	75	76	72
Republican	22	24	38	49	35	52	50	49

two bodies after 1976. Although a majority of American Catholics had identified with the Democratic Party since the New Deal, defections to the Republicans in the presidential elections occurred also in congressional elections but much more gradually (not shown here). In the Senate in 1976, there were twelve Catholic Democrats and only three Catholic Republicans. By 2000, the gap had closed to fourteen to eleven, where it remained in 2004. In 2005, Catholics are 25 percent of the Senate, about equal to their percentage in the U.S. population.

A similar pattern was found in the House. In 1976, there were eighty-two Catholic Democrats and only twenty-two Catholic Republicans (together 24 percent of the House). The Democratic numbers ranged around eighty until the 1994 and 1996 elections, when they dropped to the mid-seventies—where they have remained. Meanwhile, the numbers of Catholic Republicans more than doubled and then leveled off around fifty. Now 29 percent of House members are Catholic, more than their percentage in the total population.

One of the important findings from research on Congress is that religious affiliation tells less about a person's vote than does party membership.[2] Thus, being Catholic in Congress tells less about how the individual will vote than knowing the party to which he or she belongs. If there was ever a time when there was a unitary Catholic vote, that time has passed. There are now at least two Catholic votes, one increasingly conservative and anchored in the Republican Party and a second liberal and anchored in the Democratic Party. The differences are seen in two contrasting statements by Republican Catholic John A. Boehner of Ohio and Democratic Catholic Rosa DeLauro of Connecticut. Boehner, while running to become the House majority leader, wrote to fellow Republican House members in January 2006,

---

2. The finding was first substantiated by Benson and Williams (1982). D'Antonio and Tuch (2004) reported that 90 percent of roll-call votes in the House and Senate

I write to you today simply for the purpose of reaffirming, proudly, that I share this commitment [to protecting the lives of the unborn and ensuring that our nation's laws reflect a belief in the sanctity of life] completely, totally, and without equivocation. It is a commitment I have felt deeply throughout my life, and a commitment I will uphold unapologetically if and when I am chosen to be your next Majority Leader. As a lifelong Roman Catholic and brother to eleven siblings, I believe, and have always believed, that life begins at conception. This is not a political position I've adopted for the sake of expedience or convenience; it is part of who I am and have always been, since long before the thought of running for office had ever entered my mind.

My respect for the sanctity of life undoubtedly came, in large part, from the example set for me and my siblings by my parents. It certainly wasn't convenient for my mother to give birth to twelve children during her life. Nor was it easy for my father and mother to spend more than a decade of their adult years raising small children, and making the endless sacrifices that parenthood entails. Their sacrifices are etched upon my soul. (quoted in Chapman 2006)

By contrast, Representative Rosa DeLauro of Connecticut's Third Congressional District spoke of her commitment to her Catholic faith in a talk on October 30, 2005:

In my case, it was my lifetime of Catholic education from kindergarten through college that in no small way moved me to serve the larger community. As the daughter of immigrants growing up in New Haven's Italian neighborhood, it was the Church that bound us together as a community. My father received communion daily. Every night around my family's kitchen table, I saw how the Church could serve as the nexus between family and community, witnessing firsthand how my parents helped solve the problems of people in our neighborhood. They would both go on to serve on New Haven's City Council (DeLauro 2006).

Catholic social teachings had given each of us a commitment to the issues that have always been central to our faith, issues such as jobs, education, homelessness and protecting the environment. But perhaps more important, the Church instilled in us the idea that government had moral purpose. And for me, any discussion regarding the nexus between faith and politics must be rooted in our own understanding of government's moral responsibility to people to making opportunity real. (Consortium of Social Science Associations 2005)

These statements by two devout Catholics, one Republican and one Democrat, are important because party affiliation influences votes today more than ever. A generation ago, political parties were considered weak and a mix of often uneasy coalitions, but recent research (Fleisher 1993;

---

were now strictly along party lines; in 1972, only 34 percent were along party lines. See Broadway (2004).

Hetherington 2001; Layman and Carsey 2002) has found that as the parties have become more disciplined and more ideologically opposed, they have begun to influence the broader American public. The ideological boundaries between the two parties have sharpened into what has been called the culture wars (Hunter 1991; Pew Research Center 2006); in the process, Catholics for whom abortion has been defined as the litmus test of their orthodoxy have moved into the Republican Party, while Catholics for whom a broader respect for a woman's right to privacy and choice on abortion or matters like abortion have been drawn more and more toward the Democratic Party.

For American Catholics, the roots of the divisions in table 8.1 and exemplified in the statements by Boehner and DeLauro are found in the failure of Catholic leaders to support the late Cardinal Bernardin's effort to open a dialogue in the public square on "A Consistent Ethic of Life" as well as in the efforts of Pope John Paul II to refocus the Church's moral authority back to the Vatican, especially on sexual issues (D'Antonio et al. 1989, 1996, 2001). The divisions among Catholics are incorporated into the increasingly opposing positions taken by the two parties on issues from abortion to funds for more research on nuclear bombs, the embargo against Cuba, housing for the poor, and others. Increasingly, the votes of Catholic members of the House and Senate conform more and more to the separate party positions on these issues. In that regard, David Broder (2006, 25), one of the nation's most respected newspaper columnists, said the following with regard to the growing cohesion within the parties: "On the roll calls where the parties divided, nearly nine out of ten Republicans and Democrats voted the party line. The average House Republican was loyal 90 percent of the time; the average for House Democrats and for both parties in the Senate was 88 percent." In the 1970s, the pattern was much different. In 1972, only 34 percent of the votes in the Congress were along party lines (D'Antonio and Tuch 2004). The move toward party-line voting began in the early 1980s with the 1994 Republican congressional sweep, marking the tipping point toward party discipline and polarization. The only exception to party discipline—and it is a notable one—is that about a third of the Catholic Democrats in the House support the bishops' anti-abortion position as well as their traditional social justice teachings. There are no Catholic Republicans in either the House or the Senate whose votes are similar to this group of Catholic Democrats.

In the past five years, Republicans have been especially successful at framing issues narrowly so as to appeal to core beliefs and values. Thus, for example, the terms "family values" and "culture of life" have broad national appeal, but their content was restricted to such issues as abortion and same-sex marriage. The Republicans' understanding of family values does not include a commitment to raising the minimum wage, providing more housing for the poor and elderly, and making health insurance available to all Americans. In effect, Cardinal Bernardin's ethic of life has been redefined: the Republicans have become the guardians of a version of pro-life that focuses on opposition to abortion as a form of murder, opposition to same-sex marriage as threatening the future of the family, and support for the military, national defense, and lower taxes as a way to get more money into the hands of the individual taxpayer (Mehlman 2003).

For their part, the Democrats have taken on the mantle of a woman's right to privacy and to choice with regard to abortion. In an effort to reconcile pro-life and pro-choice Catholics within the Democratic Party, fifty-five House Democrats issued a statement of principles both to address their more traditional support for the Church's social teachings and to tie it to a nuanced statement about abortion:

> We envision a world in which every child belongs to a loving family and agree with the Catholic Church about the value of human life and the undesirability of abortion; we do not celebrate its practice. Each of us is committed to reducing the number of unwanted pregnancies and creating an environment with policies that encourage pregnancies to be carried to term. We believe this includes promoting alternatives to abortion, such as adoption, and improving access to children's healthcare and child care, as well as policies that encourage paternal and maternal responsibility.

Three bishops—the chairs of the United States Conference of Catholic Bishops Committee on Pro Life Activities, the Task Force on Catholic Politicians, and the Committee on Domestic Policy—issued a formal statement welcoming "the Representatives' recognition that Catholics in public life must act seriously and responsibly on many important moral issues." At the same time, they went on "to reaffirm the Catholic Church's constant teaching that abortion is a grave violation of the most fundamental human right—the right to life that is inherent in all human beings, and that grounds every other right we possess. . . . Above all, the common outcry, which is justly made on behalf of human rights—for example, the right to health, to home, to work, to family, to culture—is false and illusory if the right to life, the most basic and fundamental right and the condition for all other personal rights, is not defended with maximum determination. . . . Catholic teaching calls all Catholics to work actively to restrain, restrict and bring to an end the destruction of unborn human life" pp. 1–22 (United States Conference of Catholic Bishops 2006, XXX).

Gene Burns (2005) argues that the Republicans' ability to frame the abortion issue by tying it to the Catholic Church's total opposition to abortion and then raising the stakes further to talk not only about abortion as murder but also of a "culture of death" helps mobilize pro-life support but also creates an absolute barrier to any hopes for compromise between the parties. For Burns, the moral veto over compromise can severely test the limits of tolerance and civility in a pluralistic society. In that regard, the response of the bishops to the Catholic Democrats seems to leave little room for effective dialogue and engagement.

An important consequence of this struggle has been our finding that the moral authority of the bishops has been weakened for many Catholics by Church teachings on sexual issues. So also Church social justice teachings focused on the poor have been weakened for other Catholics as those Catholics embrace a more individualistic approach to the role that the Church should play in the public square. Increasingly, knowing a person is Catholic does not predict his or her attitudes on social issues. One needs to know the person's party affiliation, and, as we shall see, it is now important to know where the Catholics who call themselves Independents fall on these issues. Because our 2005 survey is our first one to include political party identification (Democrat, Republican, or Independent), we are not able to report trends over time.

A DEMOGRAPHIC OVERVIEW OF CATHOLICS BY PARTY AFFILIATION

In the 2005 survey, 39 percent of Catholics identified themselves as Republicans, 42 percent called themselves Democrats, and 19 percent said they were Independents. These figures are similar to the findings of polls and surveys taken before and after the 2004 elections. Table 8.2 shows demographic breakdowns. Thirty-eight percent of Catholic women are Republican, 45 percent are Democrats, and 17 percent are Independents. Among the men, 43 percent are Republican, 41 percent are Democrats, and 17 percent are Independents.

One in three pre–Vatican II Catholics identify themselves as Republicans, half (51 percent) call themselves Democrats, and the remaining 16 percent call themselves Independents. There is more party balance among Vatican II Catholics: 38 percent call themselves Republicans, 44 percent Democrats, and 18 percent Independents. The more dramatic differences are emerging between the post–Vatican II generation and the new Millennial generation. About half of the post–Vatican II Catholics call themselves Republicans; 35 percent identify as Democrats and the rest as Independents. The figures are dramatically reversed among the youngest adult Catholics—the Millennials, with only 29 percent of them identifying as Republicans; 58 percent Democrats; and 13 percent Independents.

Voting results from the 2004 election (Niemi and Hanmer 2004; Zogby 2005) showed similar patterns: the post–Vatican II (Generation X) voters went strongly for Bush, 52 to 40 percent, while the Millennials supported

Table 8.2.   Level of Commitment in Demographic Categories, 2005 (in percentages added horizontally)

	Republican %	Democrat %	Independent %
All Catholics	39	42	19
Gender			
Female	38	45	17
Male	43	41	17
Generation			
Pre–Vatican II	33	51	16
Vatican II	38	44	18
Post–Vatican II	49	35	17
Millennials	29	58	13
Marital status			
Married	42	41	17
Living as married	52	30	17
Divorced or separated	54	26	20
Widowed	23	61	16
Never married	29	55	16
Education			
High school graduate or less	37	48	15
Some college, vocational, or technical training	39	43	18
College graduate	46	33	21
Graduate, professional degree	38	47	15
Household income			
Less than $30,000	32	53	15
$30,000–$50,000	45	37	18
$50,000–$75,000	40	40	20
$75,000 or more	41	34	25

Kerry 56 to 43 percent. We will have to wait until our 2011 survey of Catholics to find out whether the swing of Millennial Catholics toward the Democrats is a long-term trend or only an indication that these young Catholics are still trying to sort out their political identities.

Insofar as marital status may reflect family values, there is little to distinguish among Democrats, Republicans, and Independents. The larger number of Democrats who have never been married may well reflect their larger numbers among the Millennials, with the average age at marriage increasing each year.

Table 8.2 shows that Republicans are more likely to have had a college education and that almost half the respondents with a high school or less formal education were Democrats. Some of this difference is probably found in the higher percentages of older Catholics among the Democrats. Regarding family income, the differences between parties are most noteworthy at the lowest income level. The lower the income level, the more respondents said they were Democrats.

Not to be overlooked in this table are the Independents: they are equally likely to be male and female and also rather evenly distributed across generations while a bit more likely to be college graduates.

These findings reveal many of the conditions that have come to characterize the two parties more generally. Other studies confirm that Catholic women are more Democratic than Republican, and women are the majority in both parties now—as they are in the country as a whole. Democrats are older, Republicans are younger, and the new Millennial generation is still in question.

CATHOLIC IDENTITY AND PARTY POLITICS

Our surveys over time have shown that Catholics agree on a number of beliefs as central or core to their identity as Catholics and that they perceive other teachings as more peripheral. Is this as true among Catholic Republicans and Catholic Democrats? Table 8.3 provides some insights. At the top of the table are four creedal beliefs that are widely seen as central, and 70 percent or more of party members are in agreement across party lines. These are belief in Jesus' resurrection from the dead, helping the poor, the Eucharist, and Mary as the Mother of God. Nine out of ten Republicans gave their strongest emphasis to the belief in Jesus' resurrection, while nine of ten Democrats gave their strongest support to the belief in the importance of helping the poor.

More than half of the Republicans saw daily prayer life, devotions like the Rosary, and opposition to abortion and same-sex marriage as very important. Democrats were significantly less likely to see saying the Rosary and similar devotions, opposition to abortion, and opposition to same-sex marriage as very important parts of their faith as Catholics. Consonant with those beliefs was the finding that half the Republicans but only 37 percent of the Democrats saw the teaching authority claimed by the Vatican as very important to them. The Independents were located between the two party groups on most of the items, but they were significantly less likely than the Republicans to say that opposition to same-sex marriage, opposition to abortion, and the teaching authority of the Vatican were very important to them.

All three political groupings were in basic agreement on other attitudes, such as "How a person lives is more important than their being Catholic," "Being Catholic is a very important part of who they are," and that they

Table 8.3. Importance of Catholic Beliefs and Practices, by Party Affiliation (in percentages)

	All %	Republican %	Democrat %	Independent %
Beliefs and practices very important to me:				
Jesus' resurrection from the dead	84	91	79	82
Helping the poor	84	81	89	84
The Eucharist	76	79	75	71
Mary as Mother of God	74	78	70	78
Participating in devotions (e.g., Rosary)	50	57	45	51
Teachings opposing same-sex marriage	47	57	41	37
Regular daily prayer life	54	56	52	50
Teachings opposing abortion	44	56	36	34
Teaching authority claimed by Vatican	42	50	37	35
Church involvement in social justice	47	45	49	43
Having a celibate male clergy	29	35	29	20
Catholic Church teachings opposing the death penalty	35	34	39	29

could not imagine themselves being anything but Catholic (not shown in the table; see chapter 2).

With regard to what it takes to be a "good Catholic" (not shown in the table), the parties differed on two items, with two out of three Republicans (65 percent) but only half the Democrats (54 percent) saying that you can be a good Catholic without donating time or money to help the poor; the percentages were reversed on the item "without obeying the Church hierarchy's teaching on abortion." The Independents were in the middle (57 percent) on both items.

The laity agreed across party lines that they had a right to participate in Church governance matters. They differed only in their degree of support for the laity's right to participate in deciding whether women should be ordained: a majority of Republicans (58 percent) agreed they should; two out of three Democrats and Independents agreed. On the Church Commitment Index, Republicans, Democrats, and Independents were similar. That is, all three have equal commitment to the institutional Church.

PARTY AFFILIATION AND THE LOCUS
OF MORAL AUTHORITY

The questions about the locus of moral issues we explored since 1987 continue to be heated today among Catholics and in the larger society, as the 2004 election showed. Table 8.4 displays the results from the 2005 survey, as seen by the Catholic Republicans, Democrats, and Independents. Here is a summary:

1. Republicans were the most likely to see Church leaders as the proper locus of moral authority on four of the five issues, with a high of 37 percent on the abortion question. On the fifth issue, contraceptive birth control, only 13 percent in each political group would look to Church leaders.
2. Only on the question of contraceptive birth control do a majority of

Table 8.4. Locus of Moral Authority in the Catholic Church, by Party Affiliation, 2005 (in percentages)

	Republican %	Democrat %	Independent %
Who should have the final say about what is right or wrong regarding . . .			
Divorce and remarriage without an annulment			
a. Church leaders	27	18	21
b. Individuals	35	48	41
c. Both working together	37	32	37
Practicing contraceptive birth control			
a. Church leaders	13	13	13
b. Individuals	56	63	64
c. Both working together	30	24	23
Advocating free choice regarding abortion			
a. Church leaders	37	17	21
b. Individuals	36	53	47
c. Both working together	26	29	31
A Catholic who engages in homosexual behavior			
a. Church leaders	32	18	23
b. Individuals	37	52	51
c. Both working together	29	28	24
A Catholic who has sexual relations outside marriage			
a. Church leaders	29	18	18
b. Individuals	39	51	52
c. Both working together	32	28	29

Republicans say the proper locus should rest with individual Catholics.

3. On four of the five issues, a majority of Democrats see the proper locus of moral authority to rest with individuals; only on the question of remarriage without an annulment does the percentage fall below 50 percent.

4. The second choice among Democrats was always "both laity and Church leaders working together" as the preferred way to establish moral authority on these issues. Only a minority of Democrats (less than 20 percent) would look to Church leaders on any of these issues.

5. On all five issues, Independents chose individuals as the proper source of moral authority, with the idea that Catholic laity should work with Church leaders as their second choice in all cases. Their responses on this question were in keeping with findings reported in tables 8.2 and 8.3.

PARTY AFFILIATION AND ATTITUDES TOWARD THE CHURCH'S SOCIAL TEACHINGS

We have discussed the divisions that have arisen within the two major political parties on matters relating to the Church's social teachings. The late Cardinal Bernardin had been one of the leaders in the preparation of the Peace Pastoral and the Economy Pastoral in the 1980s. After publication of these pastorals, the Government Liaison Office of the bishops lobbied on Capitol Hill on behalf of many issues raised in the pastorals (United States Conference of Catholic Bishops 2005). In recent years, however, top priority has been given to abortion, which has been declared to be the litmus-test issue for whether a politician is a good Catholic. Archbishop Raymond Burke (2003, 2004; Van Biema et al. 2004) and other bishops have even gone so far as to distinguish between the nonnegotiable issues like abortion and negotiable issues like the death penalty and housing for the poor and elderly, seeing the latter as "matters of prudent judgment."

Table 8.5 contains five items drawn from the broad array of issues that come regularly before Congress and on which the bishops' Government Liaison Office lobbies. In our survey we asked, "Following are some questions about social and political issues. Please tell me whether you strongly agree, somewhat agree, somewhat disagree, or strongly disagree." We did not indicate the position of the Catholic bishops on the issues.

The differences between the Democrats and the Republicans are significant in all five cases, as are the differences between the Republicans and the Independents. A majority of all three groups support "more government money to provide health care for poor children." Among the Republicans,

Table 8.5.   Attitudes toward Church Teachings, by Party Affiliation, 2005 (in percentages)

	Republican %	Democrat %	Independent %
Strongly agree:			
More government money to provide health care for poor children	52	81	71
More government funds for the military	50	30	37
Stiffer enforcement of the death penalty	43	22	33
Reduced spending on nuclear weapons	27	45	38
Further cutbacks in welfare programs	26	11	16

it is a bare majority (52 percent), among the Independents it is 71 percent, and among the Democrats it is a large majority (81 percent). The bishops have strongly supported more government money for this purpose.

The U.S. bishops have long lobbied against more money for the military, and Democrats have been more supportive of the bishops' position than have been the Republicans. This has led some Republican leaders like Karl Rove to declare that the Democrats are soft on defense. (In the war setting in 2006, it is difficult to carry on a debate about just how much money is needed to ensure the nation's security.) In the survey, half the Republicans but only 30 percent of the Democrats strongly supported more government funds for the military. With regard to spending for nuclear weapons, only one in four Republicans strongly supported less spending, a position that 45 percent of the Democrats supported. The bishops have opposed increased spending for the military and have advocated reducing the number of nuclear weapons.

During his papacy, John Paul II became a strong, vocal opponent of the death penalty. The U.S. bishops gradually took up the cause, speaking out both as individuals and in concert. In our 2005 survey, twice as many Republicans as Democrats (43 to 22 percent) favored stiffer enforcement of the death penalty—in opposition to the position of the bishops. On the question of cutbacks in welfare programs, only a minority of any party was in strong support, yet Republicans were twice as likely as Democrats to do so. The U.S. bishops have long been opposed to cutbacks in welfare programs.

On all five issues, the responses of the Independents were closer to the Democrats than to the Republicans.

CONCLUSION

In the course of the twentieth century, American Catholics have become part of mainstream America not only in socioeconomic matters but also in political matters. During this century, a Catholic became president of the United States, and in the U.S. House and Senate, the numbers of Catholics grew until one-quarter of the Senate and 29 percent of the House were made up of Catholics. Our survey found 42 percent of American Catholics identifying as Democrats, 39 percent as Republicans, and 19 percent as Independents—figures similar to those found in other surveys.

Despite the increasingly sharp divisions on political issues, Catholics remain in agreement on what they perceive to be the core elements of the Catholic faith. They also agree on matters having to do with the right to participate in the governance of the Church. Nevertheless, some differences among them are clear and strong, and they are differences that link Catholics' religious beliefs and attitudes with the policies of the two main parties.

Since 1980, the Republican Party has become identified as the party opposed to abortion rights and homosexuality, especially as manifested in same-sex marriage. For a significant minority of American Catholics, these have become core religious values that have also framed their political beliefs, and they have brought them to the Republican Party. Other political policies, including lower taxes and a strong military, have also attracted a growing number of Catholics to the Republican Party.

On the other side are Catholics who place the "special option for the poor" at the top of their political and religious priorities, leading them to continue to identify as Democrats. In addition, since 1980, as the Democratic Party has become the defender of *Roe v. Wade*, more and more Catholics who support the principle of a right to privacy in sexual matters have found their way into the Democratic Party. One result is the growing polarization between Catholic Democrats and Republicans.

The rhetoric surrounding issues such as abortion, same sex-marriage, and divorce and remarriage without an annulment obscures the more complex realities that our findings reveal. For example, our findings do not support the popular thesis that regular Mass attendance is the best predictor of conservative cultural politics. It appears to be party identification rather than regular Mass attendance that separates Democrats and Republicans along ideological lines. Thus, it is not as if only Democrats support more federal spending on health care for poor children any more than it is the case that only Republicans oppose abortion. Rather, the differences between them become magnified when they become part of the voting public that creates a Congress that is increasingly organized along very strongly disciplined party lines. Voting in Congress has become increasingly polarized as the

members vote more and more along party lines. One important consequence of this party discipline is that American Catholics tend to be making
party choices on the basis of a narrow selection of Catholic Church teachings that divide basically into prenatal versus postnatal expressions of
human values.

9

Conclusions: Summary and Implications

Throughout this book, we have eavesdropped on conversations between a mother and daughter from a fairly typical Catholic family. It might be expected that two members of the same family would have the same religious commitments, but they do not. The mother is a loyal and committed Catholic churchgoer, and she wishes that the daughter would take her faith more seriously and become more involved in the Church. In her words, "After all, we're Catholics, and our faith and the Church should be important to us."

The daughter, who was both baptized and confirmed in the Church, feels that she is spiritual and has a close relationship with God, but she is not registered in a parish and attends Mass only for a few special occasions. She disagrees with some things the Church does and says, and she feels she has a right to make her own religious and moral decisions. Mother and daughter came from different generations of American Catholics, which accounts for many of their differences. Catholics of the old, middle, and young generations are quite different from one another.

We have survey data documenting trends over the past eighteen years. In addition, the four of us have engaged in a number of other studies, parts of which clarify and enrich our trend data. For the present book, we saw our task as blending the available data and making sense of it all. This concluding chapter is a wrap-up of the research. First, we summarize the main research findings under eight headings, and then we state some implications of the studies as we see them.

MAIN FINDINGS

Generational Differences

The generations are clearly different in many important ways. We are not the first researchers to point this out; it has been found in every study in the past two decades. Several years ago, researchers pointed to a gap between pre–Vatican II Catholics (that is, people born in 1940 or earlier) and those born later. In our new 2003 and 2005 studies, we found divisions between pre–Vatican II Catholics and Vatican II Catholics and also between Vatican II Catholics and young adults born after about 1961.

These generational divisions help us predict the future. Within twenty years, the pre–Vatican II Catholic laity will be few in number, and they will have been replaced by the large Vatican II and post–Vatican II generations. Our 2005 survey includes some of the Millennial generation (ages eighteen to twenty-six), which will grow as younger members of this cohort reach adulthood. By looking at table 3.2, we can predict that the number of Catholics with high Church commitment will probably drop by as much as one-third. Most Catholics will continue to be in the medium-commitment category. We also can predict how lay Catholics will view Church teachings about abortion, homosexual behavior, nonmarital sex, and a celibate male clergy by looking at tables 6.2 and 6.5, which describe each generation today. In the future, Catholics will grant less authority to Church teachings and more to their own judgment.

The generational differences in this survey and other recent surveys occurred on numerous topics but not on every one. The generations were more in agreement on issues that laypeople consider central elements of the faith, such as belief in the Incarnation and Resurrection, and differed more on topics the laity consider less important, such as having a celibate male clergy. Generational differences do not exist on questions about how much the laity should be involved in Catholic decision making or in acceptance of women in most leadership roles, but they do exist on specific moral teachings about personal behavior, such as contraception.

Catholic Identity

The big picture is that most Catholics remain Catholic. Even if they are unhappy with Church leadership or Church moral teachings and even if they are disgusted with the way the bishops handled sexual abuse cases, they stay Catholic. They may attend Mass less frequently or give less to diocesan appeals, but they stay Catholic. Someone has said that with respect to maintaining their identity, Catholics in America are more like Jews than like Protestants. It seems true.

In the analysis of Catholic identity, we found that some elements of being Catholic are seen as central to the faith and others as peripheral. Everyone recognizes this to some degree. The elements people feel to be most central are helping the poor, belief in creedal statements such as Jesus' resurrection from the dead, the sacraments, and devotion to Mary as the Mother of God. As far as most Catholics are concerned, these form the unchangeable core of the faith; other things are less important and open to change.

When we asked respondents what it takes to be a "good Catholic," the answers were similar to the views of core and periphery in that belief in the creed and in the Real Presence were most important to being a good Catholic, while going to church every Sunday, obeying teachings on birth control, and having one's marriage approved by the Church were not. Since 1987, when we first studied what it takes to be a "good Catholic," these latter criteria have been seen as less and less important. The young-versus-old difference in 2005 was greatest on the importance of following Church teachings on abortion; the young people saw it as much less necessary.

What are the boundaries to the Catholic faith? Traditionally there was a single boundary between Catholics and non-Catholics. Catholics were inside, and all others were outsiders who did not have God's truth. By contrast, American Catholics today—and especially young adult Catholics—commonly see two boundaries, not one. The outer boundary defines the "tolerance zone," which includes all religions, Catholic and otherwise, which deserve respect and tolerance. When asked, Catholics tend to say that many religions are valid paths to truth. The inner boundary defines the "personal comfort zone" of churches in which the person feels comfortable. For most Catholics, the personal comfort zone includes Catholicism but not much else. These people do not feel right about switching faiths, for example, to Protestant churches. The double boundary helps explain how most American Catholics can be tolerant and respectful of other religions and at the same time maintain their own Catholic identity.

Commitment to the Church

Some Catholics are strongly committed to the Church and active in Church life; the majority are not. Older Catholics are more committed than the young. The long-term trend in level of Catholics' commitment to the institutional Church from 1987 to 2005 was moderately downward, and, on the basis of generational differences, we can predict a continued downward drift in the future.

We also learned two things about the relationship between Catholic identity and commitment to the Church. First, identity is positively correlated with commitment. It contributes to and is reinforced by commitment to the Church. Second, although the two overlap, there are still some important differences between them. Catholics are more highly aligned with the faith than they are attached to the Church. Moreover, Catholic identity is more stable than commitment to the Church. The loss in Catholic identity has not been as pronounced as the loss in commitment to the Church.

Trends in commitment are important because commitment is a strong predictor of Catholics' views on a variety of other religious issues. For example, high-commitment Catholics adhere more to creedal beliefs and devotions than other Catholics. They also are more likely to participate in and have traditional views of the sacraments. Yet high-commitment Catholics are not opposed to changes in church policies and practices. They are as likely as other Catholics to advocate more lay involvement in Catholic decision making. Overall, commitment was not as highly related to Catholics' views on political matters, but even there, it had some discernible effects. For example, highly committed Catholics are much less in favor of the death penalty than Catholics who are less attached to the Church.

The Sacraments

The 1950s was a period of unusually high participation in most sacraments. It was a period unlike anything earlier or later. For example, Mass attendance was lower in the early 1900s, and it was lower again in the 1980s and 1990s. The same inverted-U-shaped pattern describes trends for other sacraments as well, such as Confession and Holy Orders. Rather than seeing the high participation levels of the 1950s as normal and other periods as unusual (as many Catholics do), it is more accurate to see the 1950s as unusual and other periods (including the present) as more typical of the American Catholic experience.

Although fewer Catholics are attending Mass and receiving Communion on a weekly basis, a higher percentage of churchgoers are now going to Communion. This finding suggests that many people who dutifully went to Mass in the 1950s probably felt an obligation to be there and did not feel worthy to receive Communion without confession. Today, there is less social pressure to attend and more emphasis on attending because one freely chooses to do so. As a result, most of those who attend Mass these days also receive Communion.

Most Catholics continue to marry in the Church. However, attitudes of young adult Catholics about marriage and divorce point to a number of trends. More and more Catholics are choosing not to marry, those who do are increasingly marrying non-Catholics, and an increasing percentage is marrying outside the Church. As a result, the number of marriages reported by the Church is not keeping up with the growth of the Catholic population.

Problems in the Church Today

Catholics believe that the main problems in the Church today are, first of all, the sexual abuse crisis and the way it has been handled; second, the shortage of priests and sisters; and, third, the lack of young adults in Church life. The sexual abuse crisis is felt by all laity, whereas the shortage of priests and sisters and the absence of young adults are felt disproportionately by older Catholics and high-commitment Catholics.

We assessed the impact of the sexual abuse crisis, which was continually in the news for three years prior to the time of the 2005 survey, and we found that its impact was mainly on laypersons' attitudes toward bishops and higher Church authority. The impact on local parish life was small. Mass attendance, parish involvement, and financial giving have sagged but only slightly. By contrast, lay opinions about bishops became more negative, and in 2003 the majority of laity felt that the U.S. bishops were not telling the whole truth. Although attitudes toward bishops have rebounded somewhat, financial support of diocesan appeals is still suppressed, and the laity are calling for more financial accountability in the diocese.

With regard to the shortage of priests and sisters, the great majority (60 to 80 percent) of Catholics favor expanding eligibility for the priesthood to married men and to women. The highest percentage of agreement is on the option of bringing back to active service some of the priests who have resigned and married. Moreover, the percentage favoring these ways of responding to the priest shortage has grown over the past two decades.

On the problem of the low involvement of young adults in Catholic Church life, we were able to gain a clarification with these data. Young adult Catholics are committed to some aspects of the faith but not to others. They place high importance on concern for the poor, and they have strong belief on core issues such as Jesus' death and resurrection. They put the same emphasis on sacraments and daily prayer life as older Catholics. Thus, they have absorbed what many Church leaders would consider the essence of the faith and the most important Church teachings. But they are not as involved in parish life as their elders, and they are not as committed to the Church's moral teachings in the areas of gender, sex, and marriage. Our conclusion is that young adults understand the basic Christian messages of loving God and reaching out to others, but, reflecting one of the tendencies of their generation, they are only loosely connected to the Church as a religious institution.

Locus of Authority

Traditionally, the Catholic Church claimed divine authority for its doctrinal and moral teachings, and the laity agreed. Today the attitudes of laity are mixed; whether Catholics accord high authority to Church teachings varies from topic to topic. Church authority is high in the minds of the laity on creedal beliefs, the obligation to help the poor, and devotion to Mary. Acceptance of authority is lower, especially among the young, on other, more specific teachings about Church rules and moral issues, such as a celibate male clergy, opposition to the death penalty, and opposition to abortion. Many Catholics today believe that on some topics more moral authority exists in their own consciences than in Church teachings. In general, the Catholic laity trust their own consciences more on concrete moral issues, such as contraception or divorce, than on theological teachings about God and salvation.

When we asked who should have the final say about what is right or wrong on five moral issues, we found a shift from 1987 to 2005. On questions of homosexual behavior and nonmarital sex, Catholics saw less and less authority in Church teachings and more in their own consciences or in Church leaders and individuals working together. Women, more than men, shifted their view of final moral authority away from Church leaders on these two issues.

Leadership and Lay Participation

When we asked Catholic laypeople about their faith in the leadership of the U.S. bishops, their responses were quite mixed, with some expressing more confidence than others. By contrast, when we asked about the laity's confidence in parish priests, it was quite high. The distinction between national and local leadership does not appear on all questions; large majorities of the laity want better financial reporting from all levels of the Church, including reports on how much money has been spent on settling lawsuits against Church leaders.

The parish is still the place where most Catholics experience Church, and parish life is the area in which lay Catholics want more voice. Nearly all Catholic laypeople feel they should have more input into decisions about how local parish income is spent. In addition, 80 percent want input into decisions about parish closings, and 71 percent want input in selecting the priests for their parish. Almost all the laity support women in leadership positions. Support for women as priests was lower than support for women in other positions, yet in 2005, 63 percent were in favor. Overall, laypeople feel they should have more input into these decisions that affect their lives most tangibly.

Although the laity wants more involvement in decision making, the trend in attitudes of priests toward lay participation is different. Research on priests shows a decreasing interest among more recently ordained priests in collaboration with the laity and in working alongside professional lay ministers. Younger priests today are adhering increasingly to a cultic model of priesthood, which emphasizes that priests are sacramental leaders set apart from laypeople and are exemplars of holiness that are essentially different. Put simply, the trends among priests and among the laity on the topic of leadership and collaboration are in divergent directions.

Religion and Politics

We found little support for recent claims that Republicans are more religious than Democrats. For the most part, Catholic Democrats and Republicans accept the core tenets of the Catholic faith. There is not much difference between them when it comes to doctrinal issues that are grounded in the Nicene Creed and centuries of Church tradition. The two groups also had quite similar scores on our index of commitment to the Church.

There are a few differences between Catholics belonging to different parties. Catholics in the two major parties have different views of authority, with Republicans stressing the authority of the magisterium and Democrats emphasizing the authority of one's conscience. They also differ on some specific moral and political issues. For example, Republicans are more pro-life on the abortion issue; Democrats are more pro-life on issues such as health care for poor children.

But these differences are more the result of political influences than religious influences. Commitment to the Church is only loosely connected to Catholics' political choices. Highly committed Catholics are about as likely to be Democrats as they are to be Republicans. Commitment predicted differences on some other issues (such as the death penalty), but it did not do so across the board. Contrary to our expectations, commitment did not increase the likelihood that Catholics would develop views that were congruent with bishops' stances on various issues.

There has been a shift in the political identifications of Catholics. Older generations of Catholics are more likely to think of themselves as Democrats; younger generations increasingly consider themselves as independents and Republicans. However, other research shows that Catholics' voting habits have been rather volatile, not always adhering to the political parties with which they identify.

IMPLICATIONS

Finally, we come to some implications of our work. Our research team reflected at length on the findings and their meaning. The conclusions we came to are grounded in the theoretical framework we outlined in chapter

1 and that has guided our analysis throughout this book. However, they also reflect other experiences we have had in the Church over the years and some personal opinions about what seems to work and what does not. Thus, some of the ideas in this section have an editorial-like quality that we strove to keep out of earlier chapters.

The Basic Issues

Our reflections center on two fundamental issues: the sources and consequences of commitment. Along with others in the Church, we are concerned about the roots and ramifications of being attached to the Church. We too want to see Catholicism flourish and have a beneficial influence on the nation and the world. Yet the trends are not all encouraging. There are signs that commitment to the Church is weakening. There also are indications in our data that commitment to the Church has only selected effects on moral and political issues that extend beyond the Church. What can Church leaders do to enhance commitment and increase its impact?

Enhancing Commitment

Even though a majority of Catholics, including young Catholics, continue to identify with the faith, they are not as strongly committed to Church life as they used to be. Some disenchanted Catholics have left the Church completely. Estimates vary on how many, but it is widely believed that nonpracticing Catholics are now the second-largest religious group in the United States—second only to practicing Catholics. However, most Catholics have not left. They still consider themselves Catholic, but they are not as attached to the Church as previous generations have been. We have three kinds of suggestions about commitment—understanding generations, strengthening Catholic identity, and actions of leaders.

Understanding Generations

We have shown that the pre–Vatican II generation is more attached to the Church than the Vatican II generation, which is more attached than the post–Vatican II and Millennial generations. Why is this? Members of the pre–Vatican II generation grew up in the "old Church." Catholics were a lower status, marginalized group in American society. They were victims of religious prejudice and discrimination. As a result, they were highly dependent on their Church, which viewed itself as an unchanging institution, stressed the authority of Church leaders, and expected the laity to comply with Church teachings. To this day, that generation is highly committed to the Church.

Baby boomers, who are the backbone of the Vatican II generation, grew up in a different world and a different Church. By the time they were in their formative years (the 1950s and 1960s), Catholics were moving up the social ladder. Anti-Catholicism was declining, and Catholics were becoming more integrated into society—a society undergoing cultural revolution. As a result, this generation was more conflicted about its social and religious beliefs. It was not as attached to the Church as the pre–Vatican II generation and never will be.

The post–Vatican II and Millennial generations have grown up in a more white-collar society. Catholics are now squarely middle class. They have known prosperity that previous generations never knew, and they also have experienced little or no anti-Catholicism. As a result, they have not needed the Church for social protection the way the pre–Vatican II generation did. Indeed, they have experienced a Church that has taught them to take responsibility for their own faith journeys and to recognize that they have much in common with other Christians. Therefore, they are much more individualistic in their religious orientations and more inclined to think of themselves as spiritual but not religious. They are likely to do that for the rest of their lives.

The American society has had effects on each generation's commitment to the Church. The anti-Catholicism of the pre–Vatican II era limited Catholics' socioeconomic advancement and their participation in the larger society. As a result, it heightened Catholics' dependency on the Church as a safe harbor—a place to go when one needed to get out of the storm. These circumstances no longer exist. Catholics today do not need the Church as much as they used to. Younger generations of Catholics are less attached to the Church.

The wave of new immigrants presents a different challenge, one we met with European immigrants in the twentieth century. Millions of new immigrants have come, and more millions will be coming later. The U.S. bishops have created a special secretariat to reach out to them. (See appendix B.)

In the post–Vatican II era, parents and religious leaders have largely ignored—and at times even condemned—the view of the Church as an end in itself. Instead, they have stressed the view of the Church as a means of meeting members' social and spiritual needs. Today's young Catholics have learned that the Church is meaningful insofar as it helps them establish relationships with other like-minded people and contributes to their personal relationship with God. Thus, it should be no surprise that younger generations of Catholics are less committed to the Church. They do not see it as an entity to which they should commit themselves. Instead, they see it as only one of many possible means to help them meet their own needs. Some readers might describe this as a consumer mentality—emphasizing the value of shopping at the Church only when it has what the shopper is looking for. Others might describe it as a club mentality—emphasizing the value of belonging to the Church for the same reasons people join fraternities, sororities, and country clubs. These motivations, though not intrinsically religious, can be useful.

Today's young adults are more aware of the entire world than were earlier American generations. They have had more broadening experiences, such as overseas travel, than anyone in the past. They possess unprecedented means of communication readily at hand through television and the Internet. Whose middle-class extended family does not have a young adult who hasn't traveled overseas, dated young men or women of other religions, lived together with lovers without benefit of clergy, or been openly homosexual?

There is an additional influence. American leaders have been asking citizens for more tolerance, understanding, and goodwill among racial, ethnic, and religious groups, and this tolerance makes young adults more hesitant to criticize other religions as mistaken or illegitimate. As we saw in the surveys, the level of acceptance of other religions is high. Today about half of American Catholics think that Catholicism has more truth than other religions, but the other half do not. Among young adults, the vast majority do not.

If parents and Church leaders want to increase the next generation's attachment to the Church, one of the things they might do is to give renewed emphasis to the view that the Church is devoted to mission—that it has a mission that goes beyond itself while it also fulfills our social and spiritual needs. This approach can take root in any number of social contexts, including the relative prosperity and social integration of today's Catholics. As evidence, we point to Old St. Pat's Parish in downtown Chicago. Twenty years ago, it had four members. Now it has thousands. Fathers Jack Wall and John Cusick have used this mission-centered approach at Old St. Pat's and believe that it is responsible for the parish's remarkable growth. The new members include many prosperous young adult Catholics—proving that Old St. Pat's is compatible with the values and interests of the post–Vatican II and Millennial generations. As members have committed themselves to the mission of the Church, their social and spiritual needs have been met, and as their needs are met, they have recommitted themselves to the mission of the Church.

Mission trips and service-learning experiences are other examples of opportunities to experience the Church in mission. Hands-on projects, such as rebuilding storm-damaged houses, preparing and serving meals in a soup kitchen, and working with poor children in an after-school mentoring program, help young people to see beyond their own needs and desires. They learn to connect the mission of the Church with their own actions in service to others. And they learn that in serving others they find personal and spiritual fulfillment. We believe these opportunities can and should be expanded.

We also believe that more effort should be put into supporting small Christian communities, such as study groups, faith-sharing groups, and prayer groups. They can strengthen commitment and connect the younger generation to the riches of Catholicism. We have experienced impressive small Christian communities on certain college campuses and find them hopeful for the Church. Research has shown that in parish life, small Christian communities are one of the dynamic areas of growth (Lee and D'Antonio 2000).

Strengthening Catholic Identity

Catholic identity, as we have shown, is strongly correlated with commitment to the Church. Thus, an increase in Catholics' identification with the Catholic faith can help to increase commitment to the Church.

How can Church leaders increase Catholic identity? One suggestion is to focus attention on the core elements and distinctiveness of the Catholic faith. Some aspects of being Catholic are both unique and inspiring. In an experimental survey of young adults in the Washington, D.C., area, we listed eighteen ways that Catholicism is unique or nearly unique, then asked the respondents to say which ways are "sources of pride or inspiration" to them. The top four were "Catholicism has devotion to Mary the Mother of God," "Catholicism believes in the Real Presence of the body and blood of Christ," "Catholicism offers sacraments every week," and "Catholicism has a pope who speaks to world leaders, espousing Christian values and ideals." In the same survey, we asked the young people which persons in all of Church history, from the time of Jesus until now, are the most inspiring to them. The clear winners were Mother Teresa and Pope John Paul II; in third place was St. Francis of Assisi. Here we have an initial inventory of aspects of Catholicism that are both unique and inspiring.

If we were to expand this exercise to include other generations of Catholics, other names and concepts might be added to the list. Archbishop Oscar Romero, Pope Benedict XVI, Cesar Chavez, Mother Angelica, Pope John XXIII, the Berrigan brothers, St. Elizabeth Seton, Bishop Fulton J. Sheen, St. Thomas Aquinas, and Dorothy Day might also be mentioned. Other inspiring goals might include the need to close the gap between the rich and poor, the need to reduce the number of abortions, the need to work for peace in the world, and the need to reduce use of the death penalty.

Although not all Catholics would agree with each idea or person on the list, the list would call attention to the core teachings and distinctiveness of the Catholic tradition. It also would indicate the diversity of lifestyles and religious worldviews that are found within the Church. The list would pro-

vide opportunities for older and younger generations to highlight the people and ideas that are most important to them and would invite people on
the religious right and religious left to acknowledge one another's icons.

If the Church were to celebrate these ideas, heroes, and heroines even
more than it does at present, there is a good chance that its efforts would
lead to even greater identification with the faith. Because one's self-concept
has behavioral implications, it is quite likely that people with elevated
awareness of Catholicism's distinctiveness would seek opportunities to participate in the Church. By demonstrating how the Church has supported
these ideas and how important a role it has played in the lives of these
heroes and heroines, Church leaders will have planted seeds that are likely
to result in heightened levels of commitment.

Actions of Church Leaders

A third suggestion involves the actions of Church leaders, both clerical
and lay. As occupants of highly visible leadership roles, these people have
extraordinary opportunities to influence the thinking of the laity, including
laypeople's commitment to the Church.

We have shown that laypeople have confidence in most local priests. By
and large, they believe their parish priests are doing a good job. When conversations turn to people they admire and respect, many laypeople mention
particular priests they have known over the years. In some parishes, there
are priests and sisters who are considered to be almost saintly, usually
because of their exceptional personalities and their selfless efforts on behalf
of their parishes. We have no doubt that these role models contribute to
the laity's commitment to the Church: "If he or she can love the Church
that much, then it should be an important part of my life too."

Yet our surveys also show that Church leaders' behaviors can have detri-
mental effects. Laypeople were ashamed by reports that priests had violated
the trust and the bodies of young Catholics, and they were angry about the
way bishops mishandled these cases. The effect was an erosion of the laity's
confidence in Church leaders.

What could leaders do to restore the laity's confidence and renew its
commitment? We think it is important to work on the problems that laypeople consider the most serious challenges facing the Church. According
to the data presented in chapter 5, these challenges are to put an end to the
sexual abuse of children by priests, to make sure that bishops handle any
future cases of abuse more swiftly and effectively, to address the growing
shortage of priests, and to increase young adults' participation in the
Church. If leaders focus their attention on addressing these problems, laypeople are likely to respond with renewed confidence in their leaders. But
if leaders give their attention only to issues that laypeople consider unimportant, the laity will become more cynical and alienated from the Church.

Another suggestion is to respond to the laity's desire to be involved in decisions at virtually all levels of Church life (see chapters 6 and 7). A priority area is sexual and reproductive ethics. Fewer and fewer laypeople believe that clergy alone should have the final say on matters such as homosexuality, the ordination of women, abortion, and contraception. Increasingly, laypeople believe that clergy and laypeople should share in decisions related to such matters. To the extent that leaders ignore the laity's desire to think about these issues in dialogue with theologians, bishops, and other officials, they are likely to diminish the laity's attachment to the Church. On the other hand, if they reach out to laypeople, seek their input, and take it seriously (as they did in the 1983 peace pastoral and the 1986 pastoral letter on economic justice), they would take an important step toward bringing laypeople into greater union with the Church. Doing so would also be consistent with the Vatican II document *Lumen Gentium* (Light of the Nations), chapter 12, which says, "The body of the faithful as a whole, anointed as they are by the Holy One (cf. Jn. 2:20,27), cannot err in matters of belief. Thanks to a supernatural sense of the faith which characterizes the People as a whole, it manifests this unerring quality, when, from the bishops down to the last member of the laity, it shows universal agreement in matters of faith and morals" (Abbott 1966, 29).

Related to this is the laity's involvement in issues related to personnel, finances, and Church management. Most clergy will admit that these are time-consuming responsibilities that have little to do with the sacramental and pastoral work that is at the core of their ministries. Meanwhile, highly educated, professional laypeople who have expertise in these areas are volunteering to serve, often at considerable personal cost. Canon law calls for a finance council for each parish and recommends a parish pastoral council as well. Many pastors are implementing these consultative bodies in parishes and learning a more collaborative leadership style. More than 30,000 lay ecclesial ministers now serve on parish staffs, many of them assisting with parish management tasks. The more the laypeople are involved, the stronger will be their commitment to the Church.

All of these efforts require dialogue between generations, as younger and older Catholics work together to negotiate issues and solutions. They also help to bridge the communication gap that now exists between liberals and conservatives. In addition, they help clergy and laity work together on topics that are of mutual concern and solutions that address the common good.

Increasing Commitment's Impact

As we showed in several chapters, commitment to the Church affects Catholics' views of important Church issues. It does not guarantee agreement with all Church teachings, but it does increase the laity's tendency to comply. It has less effect on religious issues that laypeople view as peripheral or optional, and it has only limited impact on issues that extend into areas of public policy and partisan politics. How can Church leaders influence committed Catholics to support Church teachings, especially on issues that go beyond parish walls and diocesan boundaries?

Leaders, for starters, might address each of the components of our Commitment Index. That is, they might try to make the Church a more important part of laypeople's lives, convince them that belonging to the Church is a lifetime commitment, and persuade them to participate in the Church (such as going to Mass on a weekly basis). How? Coercion is not possible in the context of America's culture of individualism and choice. Admonition is not likely to get a good response either. The only way is persuasion.

Under what conditions does persuasion work? We emphasize two conditions. First, calls by leaders work when the message appeals to people's most central values—the things that they consider right and good. When their most central values are at stake, people of different generations, different theological orientations, and different statuses in the Church will listen and will be predisposed to act. Their consciences will have an effect. If not, people will not be persuaded. Second, persuasion works when the message appeals to people's self-interests. If people have something to gain from the message, they will be inclined to act. If the message contains more costs than benefits, people will be far less enthusiastic. Church leaders are most persuasive when both of these conditions are met. When one of these conditions is missing, the laity is not as likely to be persuaded. When both are missing, leaders will have virtually no impact on the laity's thoughts and actions. Stated differently, Church leaders are most likely to persuade laypeople to comply with church teachings and to apply these teachings to their worldly concerns when they are able to show that doing so is the right thing for laypeople to do and that doing so would improve the quality of their lives. To date, leaders have been most successful in persuading Catholics that adhering to the core teachings of the Church is consistent with both their values and their interests.

Church leaders have been less successful in several other areas that laypeople consider less important. These includes rules governing religious practices (for example, that Catholics should go to Mass at least once a week, go to Confession at least once a year, and get married in the Church). Neither have Church leaders been successful in persuading Catholics to conform to the Church's stances on sexual and reproductive issues or on selected social issues, such as rights of homosexuals or support of labor unions. Our analysis suggests either that leaders have failed to convince Catholics that these teachings are right or that they have failed to show how complying with these teachings would improve the laity's lives.

An impressive finding is that trends among committed Catholics are away from support for the death penalty. This issue is one on which the American bishops have labored hard and invested much money. It exemplifies what effect Catholic teaching can have on an issue defined to be non-dogmatic and open to dialogue.

We would encourage dialogue about both the need for laypeople to modify their values and interests and also the need for the Church to reformulate its views on topics where laypeople are in most disagreement. Probably Church leaders might be most inclined to stress the first course of action; laypeople might favor the second. To avoid an impasse, leaders might try to identify teachings that could be modified without damaging the core elements of the faith, and laypeople might try to identify those values and interests that they are most willing to adjust for the sake of being in greater compliance with the Catholic tradition. These modifications might increase the Church's impact on the laity's attitudes and behaviors both inside and outside the Church.

Dialogue over the death penalty is an example; the efforts of the Church have had a good effect on American attitudes. The new dialogue over immigration reform is another example. In 2005, the U.S. Bishops launched a campaign, "Justice for Immigrants," to advocate for comprehensive immigration reform. A number of bishops have been speaking out on the moral issues involved. The campaign appeals to a range of ages through use of media, it clearly links the issue to scripture and to Catholic social teaching, and it asks Catholics to take part in grass-roots advocacy efforts. It is engaging Catholics and non-Catholics of all political viewpoints.

This volume is the fourth in a series that has documented trends among American Catholics. We have identified continuities on matters that are central to the faith and the Church, and we have monitored changes in less central areas. Commitment to the Church is in gradual decline. We have explored some conditions contributing to this decline and have offered some proposals for addressing the situation. We also have identified areas where commitment does not have the consequences that one might expect it to have.

We hope and pray for a vibrant Church and a Church that is a blessing for the entire society. We hope that this book will serve as a means for dialogue in the Church. Just as our mother and daughter have done throughout the pages of this book, we hope that lay Catholics of different generations, different levels of commitment to the Church, and different viewpoints will come together to talk about what the faith and the Church mean to them. If this book helps to increase dialogue in the Church, it will have served its purpose well.

Appendix A

Catholic Education

Catholic school closings are a concern for many Catholics today. American Catholics have a long history of support for Catholic education for young people. In 1884, the Third Plenary Council of Baltimore mandated that every parish build a parish school (Froehle and Gautier 2000, 65). Thousands of Catholic elementary and high schools were built in the first half of the twentieth century—half of all Catholic elementary schools in existence today were built before 1948—primarily in areas that had the greatest concentration of Catholics at the time (Gray and Gautier 2006). However, even at their peak in the 1950s, no more than half of all parishes had a school, and fewer than half of all Catholic children were enrolled in a Catholic elementary school. Today, those areas that once had the greatest concentration of Catholics and the highest number of Catholic parishes and schools are now losing population entirely, or in some cases the Catholic population is being replaced by other groups. Eight in ten Catholic elementary schools that closed between 2000 and 2005 were in the Middle Atlantic or the Great Lakes regions—areas that still include more than half (55 percent) of all Catholic schools in operation today (Gray 2006).

Partly as a result of this twentieth-century movement of Catholics from the urban centers of the Northeast and the farms and towns of the upper Midwest to the Sunbelt, the Southwest, and the suburbs, Catholics of different generations have had somewhat different access to Catholic schools. While more than half of all Catholics (54 percent) in the 2005 survey attended Catholic schools and each generation averages about eight years of Catholic education, Vatican II Catholics are more likely than those of other generations to have attended a Catholic elementary school or a Catholic high school (see table A.1). This generation, which roughly corresponds to the baby boom, had access to Catholic education at a rate not experienced in generations before or since their time.

Table A.1.   Did You Ever Attend a Catholic School or College for Any of Your
Education?, 2005 (percentage responding "yes")

	Generations			
	Total %	*Pre–Vatican II* %	*Vatican II* %	*Post–Vatican II* %
Attended a Catholic elementary school	49	42	59	45
Attended a Catholic high school	29	22	33	29
Attended a Catholic college or university	12	11	13	12
Average number of years of Catholic education (among those attending Catholic schools)	8.25	8.97	8.68	7.66

Does Catholic education actually make a difference in people's lives? The question on many Catholics' minds is whether attending Catholic schools has a unique effect on young people. Is it better academically? Does it produce stronger Catholic identity? To provide answers to such questions, a researcher needs to compare graduates of Catholic schools with other Catholic youth, then measure and control for other influences on the former to isolate the specific effects of Catholic schooling. After all, children who attend Catholic schools are not a random sample of all Catholic youth. Parents of children in Catholic schools tend to be more active in parish life than parents whose children do not attend Catholic schools. Tuition and other school costs make Catholic schooling prohibitive for some families. As a result of these and other factors, students in Catholic schools are different from other students, even before their school experiences.

A number of prominent research studies have attempted to measure the effects of Catholic schooling by comparing Catholic school graduates with other youth after statistically removing other significant influences on the youth. We cannot do the same here; our brief survey did not gather this background information because our purposes were wider. We can report how Catholic school graduates are different from other adult Catholics on the questions we asked, but this does not prove that Catholic schooling alone produced those differences. The most we can do here is to point out the findings of some other controlled studies of Catholic school effects.

ATTACHMENT TO THE CHURCH

Existing research on Catholic schooling and religious commitment has shown mixed results. Early studies, particularly those conducted by Andrew

Greeley and his colleagues, presented positive effects of Catholic schooling on many religious practices and beliefs of Catholic adults (Brown and Greeley 1970; Greeley and Rossi 1966; Greeley et al. 1976). A comparative analysis of data from public and private schools by James Coleman and colleagues concluded that students from Catholic schools performed better academically than their counterparts in public schools regardless of parental backgrounds (Coleman et al. 1982). Later research explained how it is that Catholic high schools contribute to "a more equitable social distribution of achievement" Bryk et al. 1993, 298). We have found limited effects of Catholic schooling on Catholics' beliefs and practices in the previous studies in this series—even without controlling for background differences (D'Antonio et al. 1989, 1996, 2001). In general, we have found a relationship between greater levels of Catholic education and both higher commitment to the Church and less reliance on Church authority in moral decision making (D'Antonio et al. 1996; Davidson et al. 1997).

LEVELS OF CATHOLIC EDUCATION

We need to know *which levels* of Catholic education a person had. Simply asking total years of Catholic education does not yield sufficient information. Two people with nine total years of Catholic schooling may have had very different experiences. One may have attended Catholic schools from kindergarten through eighth grade and then gone on to public schools. Another may have first attended Catholic schools by enrolling in a Catholic high school and then completing one or two degrees in a Catholic college or university. Their total years of Catholic education are the same, but their experiences were very different. We were able to examine those differences in this study by asking not only how many total years of education in Catholic schools a person has had but also whether he or she had attended a Catholic elementary school, a Catholic high school, or a Catholic college or university.

Figure A.1 shows that for more than half of those who attended a Catholic elementary school, that is where their Catholic schooling ended—they completed eight or fewer years of Catholic schooling. About half of those who attended a Catholic high school (middle bar) completed nine to twelve years of Catholic schooling, most likely because they attended a Catholic elementary school first. However, more than a quarter of those who attended a Catholic high school did not go all the way through Catholic elementary and high school because they completed eight or fewer years of Catholic schooling. Finally, more than a third of those who attended a Catholic college or university completed eight or fewer years of Catholic schooling—demonstrating that they did not complete both Catholic elementary and high schools, if in fact they attended either one. A plurality (42 percent) of Catholics who attended a Catholic college completed all or most of their education in Catholic schools, but more than half did not.

Attending a Catholic elementary school, however, does increase the likelihood that one will go on to attend a Catholic high school (not shown in the figure). More than half (52 percent) of those who attended a Catholic elementary school went on to attend a Catholic high school. Among those who attended a Catholic high school, nearly nine in ten (89 percent) said they also had attended a Catholic elementary school. Nearly as many Catholic college or university attendees (79 percent) said they had attended a Catholic elementary school, and about two-thirds (65 percent) had attended a Catholic high school.

CONSIDERATION OF A VOCATION

Is Catholic education related to consideration of a vocation? About one in five lay Catholics say they have considered a vocation to priesthood or religious life. Among Catholic men who attended a Catholic elementary school, 29 percent said they had considered becoming a priest or a brother (compared with 13 percent who had not attended a Catholic elementary school). For Catholic women who attended a Catholic elementary school, 23 percent said they had considered becoming a sister or a nun (compared

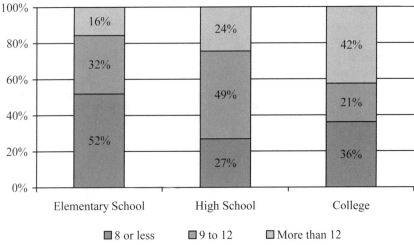

Figure A.1.   Total Years of Catholic Schooling, by Level of Catholic Schools Attended

with 13 percent who had not attended). For those who attended a Catholic high school, 35 percent of men and 27 percent of women (compared with 16 percent of men and 14 percent of women who had not attended) said they had considered a religious or priestly vocation (Center for Applied Research in the Apostolate 2003). Taken together, 60 percent of those who attended a Catholic elementary school and 67 percent of those who attended a Catholic high school said they would encourage someone to become a priest, nun, sister, or brother.

Among Catholic priests, 75 percent attended a Catholic elementary school, and 68 percent attended a Catholic high school. Post–Vatican II priests are more likely than lay Catholics of that same generation to have attended Catholic schools. Nearly six in ten (59 percent) post–Vatican II generation priests, compared with 45 percent of post–Vatican II lay Catholics, attended a Catholic elementary school. Likewise, 49 percent of post–Vatican II priests, compared with 29 percent of post–Vatican II lay Catholics, attended a Catholic high school.[1]

We cannot say that attendance at a Catholic elementary school predisposes one to priesthood or a religious vocation because Catholic school graduates also had other influences on their lives. A recent survey of seminarians who were being ordained in 2006 found that they are no more likely than other Catholics to have attended a Catholic elementary school (52 percent of ordinands compared with 49 percent of U.S. Catholics overall and 45 percent of post–Vatican II Catholics). But the seminarians are more likely than U.S. Catholics in general to have attended a Catholic high school (43 percent of ordinands compared to 29 percent of U.S. Catholics).[2]

TRENDS IN CATHOLIC ELEMENTARY SCHOOLS

So far, we have seen that those who attended Catholic schools differ in some Catholic attitudes and behaviors from those who did not attend. Although those differences are more pronounced among persons who attended Catholic high schools or colleges, the greatest single predictor of attendance in higher-level Catholic institutions is Catholic elementary

---

1. The figures on post–Vatican II generation Catholic priests are from the Center for Applied Research in the Apostolate (2002). The figures on post–Vatican II generation lay Catholics are from the 2005 Gallup survey for this project.

2. Statistics on ordinands are from "The Class of 2006," a report authored by Mary Gautier and Mary Bendyna, RSM, of the Center for Applied Research in the Apostolate for the U.S. Conference of Catholic Bishops Secretariat for Vocations and Priestly Formation. Statistics on lay Catholics are from the 2005 Gallup survey for this project.

school attendance. We have also briefly discussed the fact that changing Catholic demographics have resulted in declining enrollments in Catholic elementary schools, largely because the existing schools are located in areas of declining Catholic populations. Nevertheless, a Catholic education remains an important value for a majority of Catholics. In fact, 79 percent of Catholics in this study agreed that it is important to them that younger generations of their family grow up as Catholics. Among post–Vatican II Catholics, those who are most likely to be raising children, 81 percent agreed with that sentiment.

The Center for Applied Research in the Apostolate recently surveyed Catholic parents, pastors at parishes with elementary schools, and principals of Catholic elementary schools as part of a major study of trends in Catholic elementary school enrollments (Gray and Gautier 2006). The survey of parents asked them to rate several aspects of Catholic elementary schools according to how important each aspect was in their decision about whether to enroll their child in a Catholic elementary school. The most important aspects (rated as "very important" by more than half of Catholic parents) were quality religious education, a safe environment, quality academic instruction, discipline and order, and a sense of community.

Pastors and principals were also asked to rate the same set of aspects according to how important they think each is to parents who send their children to the school. The research found a difference between what parents think is "very important" in a Catholic education and what school leaders perceive is important for parents. More than eight in ten parents said that quality religious education was a very important aspect, but only about two-thirds of school leaders saw that as a very important aspect for parents. The principals and pastors were more likely to say that a safe environment, quality academic instruction, discipline and order, affordable tuition, a sense of community, and up-to-date classroom technology were "very important" for parents. They underestimated the importance that parents place on a quality religious education for their children.

Whether this desire for a quality religious education for their children among Catholic parents is sufficient to mobilize the capital necessary to construct new Catholic elementary schools in the places where the Catholic population now live is an open question. Our research shows that nearly eight in ten Catholics say it is important to them that the younger generations of their family grow up as Catholics. The decision as to whether Catholic parents will continue to have the option to send their children to Catholic schools rests in the hands of Catholics today; it is a financial issue.

At their June meeting in 2005, the U.S. Catholic bishops approved a document titled *Renewing Our Commitment to Catholic Elementary and Secondary Schools in the Third Millennium*. It affirms the need to offer "the future leaders of our Church" a Catholic education but admitted that there are many challenges entailed in carrying out this goal. The document also pointed out the valuable role played by Catholic schools, particularly for students from poorer families and minority groups. "Catholic schools have a lower dropout rate (3.4 percent) than both public (14.4 percent) and other private schools (1.9 percent). And 99 percent of Catholic high school students graduate, with 97 percent going on to some form of post-secondary education. Catholic school students also score well on standardized tests, surpassing standards established by federal and state agencies" (United States Conference of Catholic Bishops 2005, 6).

Appendix B

Hispanic Catholics

In this appendix, we explore differences between Hispanic[1] Catholics and other Catholics. We asked Gallup to include an oversample of 175 Hispanic Catholics in the 2005 survey so that we could compare Hispanics with all other Catholics. The number of Hispanic Catholics is constantly growing, and this will be important in the future. The sample of Hispanic Catholics who were interviewed for this survey is not representative of all Hispanic Catholics in the United States, for several reasons. First, the survey was conducted entirely by telephone. Hispanics, especially recent immigrants, are less likely than the general population to have a telephone number. Second, recent immigrants and undocumented persons are more likely than others to live in multifamily households and are underrepresented because the interviewer asks to interview only one person in the household. Finally, Spanish-speaking Hispanics are less likely than those whose native language is English to be comfortable answering questions in English. (For an analysis of systematic bias in surveys of Hispanic Catholics, see Perl et al. 2004.)

According to U.S. Census figures, the Hispanic population in the United States grew from 22.3 million in 1990 to 42.7 million in 2005, an increase of 91 percent (U.S. Census Bureau, 2006). During the same time period, the non-Hispanic population in the United States grew by 12 percent (from 226.4 million to 253.7 million). Thus, Hispanics now make up 14 percent of the total U.S. population, surpassing blacks as the largest nonwhite population group in the United States.

---

1. For the sake of brevity, we use the generic term "Hispanic" here to refer to all persons of Hispanic origin or descent. In our 2005 survey, these would include all Catholics who answered yes to the question "Are you, yourself, of Hispanic origin or descent, such as Mexican, Puerto Rican, Cuban, Honduran, Dominican, Salvadoran, or other Hispanic of Latino background?"

The Census Bureau is prohibited by law from asking questions about religious identification, so researchers rely on telephone surveys to estimate the proportion of Hispanics who are Catholic. Estimates range from just over half to nearly 90 percent, but an analysis by the Center for Applied Research in the Apostolate of eleven national surveys conducted since 1990 suggests that approximately 70 percent of Hispanics self-identify as Catholic (Perl et al. 2004). Because the Hispanic population is younger than the U.S. population as a whole and because it is a rapidly growing group, the proportion of U.S. Catholics who are Hispanic will continue to swell in the near future.

DEMOGRAPHICS OF U.S. HISPANIC CATHOLICS

Although the Hispanic Catholics interviewed for this survey are not representative of all U.S. Hispanic Catholics for the reasons cited here, they are still a useful comparison group and can illustrate some important demographic changes.

For example, when we examine the ethnic and racial identification of each of the four generations of U.S. Catholics in our survey, we see how diverse the Church is becoming. Pre–Vatican II and Vatican II Catholics (those aged forty-five and older), who now make up only about half of all adult Catholics in the U.S. Church, are overwhelmingly non-Hispanic white. Post–Vatican II Catholics, between the ages of twenty-seven and forty-four in 2005 (four in ten of all adult Catholics in the United States) are much more likely than the generations before them to be something other than white, non-Hispanic. One in five is Hispanic. The diversity is even more striking in the Millennial generation, where just over half are non-Hispanic white and four in ten are Hispanic (see figure B.1).

With our survey, we can compare Hispanic Catholics with other Catholics. The Hispanic Catholics interviewed in English for this survey are most likely the children, grandchildren, and great-grandchildren of immigrants to the United States. They are more fully assimilated into American culture than are Spanish-speaking Hispanic Catholics, and they share many of the characteristics of non-Hispanic Catholics. These Hispanic Catholics are almost evenly distributed between males and females. They are younger than non-Hispanics, with an average age of thirty-nine, compared with forty-nine for non-Hispanic Catholics. In terms of Catholic generations, Hispanic Catholics are clearly younger.

There is virtually no difference between the Hispanics and non-Hispanics in education. In both groups, approximately a third has only a high school education, another third has completed some college, and another third has finished a college degree or postgraduate education. In their exposure

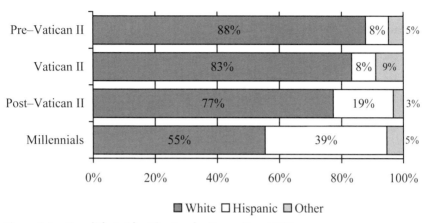

Figure B.1.   Race/Ethnic Identification by Generation, 2005

to Catholic education, non-Hispanic Catholics average just over eight years total, and Hispanic Catholics average seven and a half (not shown in table B.1). The only significant difference is in exposure to Catholic high school; non-Hispanic Catholics are more likely than Hispanic Catholics to have attended a Catholic high school (31 percent compared with 21 percent). They are equally unlikely to have attended a Catholic college or university (10 percent of Hispanic Catholics compared with 13 percent of non-Hispanic Catholics).

Hispanic Catholics are less likely to be married (61 percent compared with 72 percent of non-Hispanics) and more likely to be single and never married (24 percent compared with 14 percent). Their marriages are equally likely to have been blessed by the Church (not shown in the table). They are more likely to be located in either the South (28 percent of Hispanic Catholics compared with 16 percent of non-Hispanics) or the West (36 percent compared with 19 percent of non-Hispanics).

Hispanics are similar to non-Hispanic Catholics in household income and political party identification. In sum, the demographic picture derived from our sample shows that these Hispanic Catholics are somewhat younger than Catholics overall, more likely to be single, and more likely to live in the West or the South but otherwise remarkably similar to other Catholics.

RELIGIOUS BEHAVIOR AND ATTITUDES OF HISPANIC CATHOLICS

How do these Hispanic Catholics compare with other U.S. Catholics in their religious behavior and attitudes toward the faith? Unlike bilingual

Table B.1. Demographic Characteristics, 2005 (percentages of Hispanic and Non-Hispanic Catholics)

	Total %	Non-Hispanic %	Hispanic %
Sex			
Male	46	46	49
Female	54	54	51
Generation			
Pre–Vatican II	17	18	9
Vatican II	35	38	18
Post–Vatican II	40	38	51
Millennial	8	6	22
Education			
Less than high school	4	4	8
High school graduate	28	29	25
Some college/trade/technical training	35	35	35
College graduate	19	18	22
Postgraduate work or degree	14	15	10
Catholic education			
Elementary school	49	51	43
High school	29	31	21
College or university	12	13	10
Marital status			
Single, never married	15	14	24
Married	70	72	61
Living as married	3	3	3
Separated or divorced	6	5	9
Widowed	5	6	2
Region			
East	34	37	19
Midwest	26	28	17
South	18	16	28
West	22	19	36
Annual household income			
Under $25,000	9	9	13
$25,000 to $34,999	9	9	7
$35,000 to $49,999	18	18	20
$50,000 to $74,999	23	23	23
$75,000 to $99,999	18	17	25
$100,000 to $149,999	11	12	4
$150,000 or more	5	5	6
Political party identification			
Democrat	42	38	44
Republican	39	41	42
Independent or other	19	21	14

surveys of Hispanic Catholics living in the United States, which shows that Hispanics are less regular in their religious behavior, we find that these English-speaking Hispanic Catholics are very similar to other U.S. Catholics. They are equally as likely as non-Hispanic Catholics to be regular Mass attenders (51 percent of each group attend Mass at least one to three times a month) and to be registered in a parish (68 percent of each group).

They are no different from other Catholics in their commitment to the Church (15 percent of Hispanic Catholics compared with 22 percent of non-Hispanic Catholics score high on our measure of commitment) or in their identity as Catholics (Hispanic Catholics have a mean identity score of 4.0 compared with 3.9 for non-Hispanic Catholics). In terms of their core beliefs as Catholics, these Hispanic Catholics are nearly identical to non-Hispanic Catholics, ranking the twelve core belief statements described in chapter 2 in a similar order of importance. The only difference was that Hispanics rated "the teaching authority claimed by the Vatican" and "Church involvement in activities directed toward social justice" above "the Catholic Church's teachings that oppose same-sex marriage" and "the Catholic Church's teachings that oppose abortion." On only two of these twelve items of core beliefs were Hispanic Catholics significantly different from non-Hispanic Catholics: 67 percent of Hispanic Catholics compared with 51 percent of non-Hispanic Catholics felt that daily prayer was "very important," and 51 percent of Hispanic Catholics compared with 41 percent of non-Hispanic Catholics agreed that the teaching authority of the Vatican was "very important."

HISPANIC CATHOLICS AND PARISH LIFE

Bishops in the United States, for the most part, did not establish national parishes as a way to minister to Hispanics but preferred to minister to them from existing parishes by adding Masses in Spanish, establishing Spanish pastoral centers, and finding other ways to integrate Hispanic Catholics into parish life. According to the National Parish Inventory (NPI) of the Center for Applied Research in the Apostolate, by 2000, more than 10 percent of parishes that reported their racial or ethnic composition said that their parish was more than 40 percent Hispanic (Gautier and Perl 2000). More than one in five said they had an ethnic ministry to Hispanics or to a particular Hispanic nationality. Spanish was the most frequently reported language other than English used at Mass, and nearly a quarter of parishes reported celebrating at least one Mass a month in a language other than English. The NPI also found that parishes with at least 40 percent Hispanic parishioners were larger than majority white parishes, were faster growing (in terms of the rate of baptisms to funerals), were more likely to be pastored by a religious order priest rather than a diocesan priest, were more likely to have at least one religious sister on staff, and were more likely to have a permanent deacon on staff. On these measures of parish life, Hispanic Catholics have already had a tremendous impact on the U.S. Church.

We found that Hispanic Catholics in our 2005 survey did not differ significantly from non-Hispanic Catholics on any of the matters related to Church life that were measured in this survey, except for a few items related to parish life (see table B.2).

Assimilated Hispanic Catholics like those in this survey are relatively well integrated into parish life. Their attitudes about parish life were similar to non-Hispanic Catholics in regard to satisfaction with parish life, parish decision making, and most attitudes about ways to deal with the shortage of priests in the United States. Hispanic Catholics felt more strongly than non-Hispanics that the laity should have the right to select the priests for their parish (see table B.2). They were also more likely to agree that it would be a good thing for celibate women, such as religious sisters, to be ordained as priests. Their attitudes on all the suggested remedies for dealing with the shortage of priests (such as merging parishes, bringing in foreign priests, and closing parishes) did not differ from the attitudes of non-Hispanic Catholics, except for two items: Hispanic Catholics were more likely than non-Hispanic Catholics to say that not having a priest available for visiting the sick and having a lay parish administer were "not at all acceptable."

CONCLUSION

In summary, except for their younger ages and concentration in the West and the South, the assimilated Hispanic Catholics in our survey do not dif-

Table B.2. Attitudes about Parish Life and Parish Leadership, 2005 (percentages of Hispanic and non-Hispanic Catholics)

	Total %	Non-Hispanic %	Hispanic %
Should Catholic laity have the right to participate in selecting the priests for their parish? (percentage saying "should")	72	70	83
It would be a good thing if celibate women were allowed to be ordained as priests. (percentage saying "strongly agree")	33	32	42
Not having a priest available for visiting the sick. (percentage saying "not at all acceptable")	62	61	71
Not having a resident priest in the parish, but only a lay administrator and visiting priests. (percentage saying "not at all acceptable")	45	44	53

fer much from non-Hispanic Catholics. Although research suggests that assimilation of Hispanics is sometimes accompanied by conversion to Protestantism (Espinosa et al. 2003), those who remain Catholic tend to have very similar behaviors and attitudes to non-Hispanic Catholics. Just as we predicted more than ten years ago (D'Antonio et al. 1996, 158), Hispanic Catholics have come to resemble non-Hispanic Catholics ever more as time goes by.

Appendix C

The 2005 Gallup Survey

(Note: 875 interviews were completed. Numbers shown are weighted percentages, rounded to the next whole integer. DK/RE = don't know or refused to answer.)

1. What is your present religion?

    Catholic
    Other . . . (TERMINATE)

2. Are you currently registered as a member of a Catholic parish?

Yes	No	DK/RE
68	32	<1

3. As a Catholic, how important is each of the following to you? Would you say the following is or are very important, somewhat important, or not important at all?

	Very Important	Somewhat Important	Not at All Important	DK/RE
A. The sacraments, such as the Eucharist	76	20	4	<1
B. The Catholic Church's teachings about Mary as the mother of God	74	22	4	<1
C. Church involvement in activities directed toward social justice	47	42	10	1

173

	Very Important	Somewhat Important	Not at All Important	DK/RE
D. The teaching author-ity claimed by the Vatican	42	47	10	1
E. A celibate male clergy	29	31	39	1
F. Having a regular daily prayer life	54	37	9	0
G. Helping the poor	84	14	2	0
H. Belief in Jesus' resur-rection from the dead	84	13	3	0
I. Participating in devo-tions such as Eucha-ristic Adoration or praying the rosary	50	39	11	<1
J. The Catholic Church's teachings that oppose the death penalty	35	40	24	1
K. The Catholic Church's teachings that oppose same-sex marriage	47	25	27	1
L. The Catholic Church's teachings that oppose abortion	44	33	23	<1

4. I am going to read you some statements. For each, please tell me if you strongly agree, somewhat agree, somewhat disagree, or strongly disagree.

	Strongly Agree	Somewhat Agree	Somewhat Disagree	Strongly Disagree	DK/RE
A. How a person lives is more important than whether he or she is Catholic	68	20	6	6	<1
B. Catholicism contains a greater share of truth than other religions do	18	37	22	20	2

	Strongly Agree	Somewhat Agree	Somewhat Disagree	Strongly Disagree	DK/RE
C. Being a Catholic is a very important part of who I am	50	35	8	7	0
D. The Sacraments of the Church are essential to my relationship with God	53	29	10	8	0
E. It is important to me that younger generations of my family grow up as Catholics	46	32	15	7	<1
F. I often feel I cannot explain my faith to others	15	34	23	28	<1
G. I cannot imagine being anything but Catholic	42	28	18	12	<1

5. Next, I would like your opinion on several issues that involve the moral authority in the Catholic Church. In each case I would like to know who you think should have the final say about what is right or wrong. Is it the Church leaders such as the pope and bishops, individuals taking Church teachings in account and deciding for themselves, or both individuals and leaders working together?

	Church Leaders	Individuals	Both	Neither	DK/RE
A. A divorced Catholic remarrying without getting an annulment	22	42	35	<1	<1
B. A Catholic practicing contraceptive birth control	12	61	27	<1	0
C. A Catholic advocating free choice regarding abortion	25	44	30	<1	<1

	Church Leaders	Individuals	Both	Neither	DK/RE
D. A Catholic who engages in homo-sexual activity	24	46	28	1	<1
E. Sexual relations outside of mar-riage	22	47	30	<1	<1

6. Please indicate whether you strongly agree, somewhat agree, somewhat disagree, or strongly disagree with the following statements.

	Strongly Agree	Somewhat Agree	Somewhat Disagree	Strongly Disagree	DK/RE
A. Most priests don't expect the laity to be lead-ers, just fol-lowers	17	35	25	21	1
B. Catholic parishes are too big and imper-sonal	11	28	29	31	1
C. Catholic Church leaders are out of touch with the laity	19	44	20	16	1
D. On the whole, parish priests do a good job	52	39	6	3	<1

7. Do you support or oppose women in the following roles in the Church?

	Support	Oppose	Not Sure	DK/RE
A. Altar server	93	7	<1	0
B. Eucharistic minister	90	9	1	0
C. Deacon	81	18	1	0
D. Parish administrator	93	6	1	<1
E. Priest	63	36	1	<1

8. Following are some questions about social and political issues. Please tell me whether you strongly agree, somewhat agree, somewhat dis-agree, or strongly disagree with . . .

	Strongly Agree	Somewhat Agree	Somewhat Disagree	Strongly Disagree	DK/RE
A. More government funds to provide health care for poor children	67	25	5	3	<1
B. More government funds for the military	39	30	19	12	<1
C. Stiffer enforcement of the death penalty	32	25	19	23	1
D. Reduced spending on nuclear weapons	38	33	14	15	<1
E. Further cutbacks in welfare programs	17	23	21	38	<1

9. The following statements deal with what you think it takes to be a good Catholic. Please tell me if you think a person can be a good Catholic without performing these actions or affirming these beliefs. Can a person be a good Catholic . . .

	Yes	No	DK/RE
A. Without going to church every Sunday	76	23	<1
B. Without obeying the Church hierarchy's teaching on birth control	75	24	<1
C. Without obeying the Church hierarchy's teaching on divorce and remarriage	66	33	1
D. Without obeying the Church hierarchy's teaching regarding abortion	58	41	1
E. Without believing that in the Mass, the bread and wine actually become the body and blood of Jesus	36	63	1
F. Without their marriage being approved by the Catholic Church	67	32	<1
G. Without donating time or money to help the poor	44	56	<1
H. Without donating time or money to help the parish	58	41	<1

	Yes	No	DK/RE
I. Without believing that Jesus physically rose from the dead	23	77	0

10. For each of the following areas of Church life, please tell me if you think the Catholic laity should have the right to participate or should not have the right to participate.

	Should	Should Not	DK/RE
A. Deciding how parish income should be spent	89	11	<1
B. Deciding how diocesan income should be spent	83	16	<1
C. Selecting the priests for their parish	71	28	<1
D. Deciding about parish closings	80	19	1
E. Deciding whether women should be ordained to the priesthood	64	36	<1

11. How important is the Catholic Church to you personally?

A. The most important part of my life	11
B. Among the most important parts of my life	33
C. Quite important to me, but so are many other areas of my life	37
D. Not terribly important to me	13
E. Not very important to me at all	6
F. DK/RE	<1

12. Aside from weddings and funerals, about how often do you attend Mass?

A. At least once a week	34
B. Two or three times a month	16
C. About once a month	14
D. A few times a year	22
E. Seldom or never	14
F. DK/RE	<1

13. How regularly do you pray, apart from Mass?

A. More than once a day	15
B. Daily	48
C. Occasionally or sometimes	32
D. Seldom or never	5
E. DK/RE	<1

14. Which of the following best describes your opinion of the appropriate role for parishioners with respect to parish finances? I will read four options:

    A. Parishioners should have no role—all parish financial decisions should be made independently by the priest   3

    B. Parishioners should have general oversight, with the priest alone responsible for parish finances but reporting to parishioners   18

    C. Parishioners should have input into determining the budget, with the priest having final say   63

    D. Parishioners should have the final say over all aspects of parish finances   14

    E. DK/RE   2

15. Many dioceses have been experiencing a shortage of priests that has resulted in some changes in parish life. I am going to read a list of changes that some dioceses have made to address this shortage. Would you tell me after each if you would be willing to accept it in your parish? Would it be very acceptable, somewhat acceptable, or not at all acceptable to you?

	Very Acceptable	Somewhat Acceptable	Not at All Acceptable	DK/RE
A. Reducing the number of Masses to fewer than once a week	8	32	60	<1
B. Bringing in a priest from another country to lead the parish	43	45	11	<1
C. Not having a priest available for visiting the sick	5	32	62	<1
D. Not having a priest available for administering last rites for the dying	5	15	80	<1

16. Some dioceses have been restructuring or closing parishes. I am going to read several changes which may be recommended. Would you tell me after each if you would be willing to accept it for your parish?

Would it very acceptable, somewhat acceptable, or not at all acceptable to you?

	Very Acceptable	Somewhat Acceptable	Not at All Acceptable	DK/RE
A. Sharing a priest with one or more other parishes	39	53	8	0
B. Having a Communion service instead of a Mass some of the time	12	48	39	<1
C. Merging two or more nearby parishes into one parish	36	52	12	<1
D. Closing the parish	4	26	70	<1

17. Now I will read four statements about the priesthood. After each, would you tell me if you strongly agree, somewhat agree, somewhat disagree, or strongly disagree?

	Strongly Agree	Somewhat Agree	Somewhat Disagree	Strongly Disagree	DK/RE
A. It would be a good thing if priests who have married were allowed to return to active ministry	47	34	5	13	1
B. It would be a good thing if married men were allowed to be ordained as priests	46	29	9	15	<1
C. It would be a good thing if celibate women were allowed to be ordained as priests	33	28	9	30	<1

	Strongly Agree	Somewhat Agree	Somewhat Disagree	Strongly Disagree	DK/RE
D. It would be a good thing if married women were allowed to be ordained as priests	31	23	9	36	1

18. On a scale from one to seven, with "1" being "I would never leave the Catholic Church" and "7" being "Yes, I might leave the Catholic Church," where would you place yourself on this scale?

Point	1	2	3	4	5	6	7	DK/RE
Percentage	42	13	11	10	10	6	8	0

Now a few questions just for statistical purposes:

19. MARITAL STATUS: Are you currently married, divorced, or have you never been married?

Married	70
Living as married	3
Separated	<1
Divorced	6
Widowed	5
Never married	15
DK/RE	<1

20. If married, was your current marriage approved by the Catholic Church as a valid marriage?

Yes	73
No	26
DK/RE	1

21. EDUCATION: What is the highest level of education you have completed?

Less than high school graduate (0–11)	4
High school graduate (12)	28
Some college	29
Trade/technical/vocational training	6
College graduate	19
Postgraduate work/degree (academic or professional)	14
DK/RE	<1

22. Did you ever attend a Catholic school or college for any of your education?

	Yes	No	DK/RE
A. Attended Catholic elementary school	49	51	<1
B. Attended Catholic high school	29	71	<1
C. Attended Catholic college or university	12	88	<1

23. How many TOTAL years of education did you receive in Catholic schools? (Percentages include only those who did attend a Catholic school. In all, 45 percent reported 0 years in Catholic schools.)

Years	1–2	3–4	5–6	7–8	9–10	More than 10	DK/RE
Percentage	13	13	11	20	7	36	<1

Mean years of Catholic schooling   8.3
Median years of Catholic schooling   8

24. ETHNICITY: Are you yourself of Hispanic origin or descent, such as Mexican, Puerto Rican, Cuban, Honduran, Dominican, Salvadoran, or other Hispanic or Latino background?

Yes	15
No	85

25. RACE: What is your race? Are you . . .

White, Anglo, or Caucasian non-Hispanic	79
Hispanic	15
Black or African American	3
Asian, Native Hawaiian, or other Pacific Islander	2
American Indian or Alaskan Native	1

26. GENDER:

Male	46
Female	54

27. AGE: What year were you born? (RECODED INTO YEARS OF AGE)

Years	18–34	35–49	50–64	65+
Percentage	27	30	26	17

Mean years of age   47
Median years of age   45

28. GENERATION:

Pre–Vatican II (65–96)	17
Vatican II (45–64)	35
Post–Vatican II (27–44)	40
Millennial (18–26)	9

29. REGION:

East	34
Midwest	26
South	18
West	22

30. PARTY: Generally speaking, do you usually think of yourself as a Republican, a Democrat, an Independent, or what?

Democrat	42
Republican	39
Independent	16
Some other party	3
DK/RE	<1

31. INCOME: What is your total annual *household* income before taxes:

Under $25,000	9
$25,000 to $34,999	9
$35,000 to $49,999	18
$50,000 to $74,999	23
$75,000 to $99,999	18
$100,000 to $149,999	11
$150,000 or over	5
DK/RE	6

References

Abbott, Walter M. 1966. *The Documents of Vatican II*. New York: Herder and Herder.

Allen, John. 2004. *All the Pope's Men*. New York: Doubleday.

Alwin, Duane. 1984. Trends in Parental Socialization Values: Detroit, 1958–1983. *American Journal of Sociology* 90: 359–82.

———. 1986. Religion and Parental Child-Rearing Orientations: Evidence of a Catholic-Protestant Convergence. *American Journal of Sociology* 92, no. 2: 412–40.

Bausch, William J. 1989. *Pilgrim Church: A Popular History of Catholic Christianity*. Mystic, Conn.: Twenty-Third Publications.

Beal, John. 2004. Constitutionalism in the Church. In *Governance, Accountability, and the Future of the Catholic Church*, edited by Francis Oakley and Bruce Russett. New York: Continuum.

Benson, Peter L., and Dorothy L. Williams. 1982. *Religion on Capitol Hill: Myths and Realities*. San Francisco: Harper and Row.

Bianchi, Eugene, and Rosemary Ruether. 1992. *A Democratic Catholic Church*. New York: Crossroad.

Bliss Institute. 2004. *Fourth National Survey of Religion*. Akron, Ohio: Akron University.

Broadway, Bill. 2004. In Congress, Religion Drives the Divide. *Washington Post*, August 27, B6–B7.

Broder, David. 2006. United in Division. *Washington Post*, January 26, 25.

Brown, William E., and Andrew M. Greeley. 1970. *Can Catholic Schools Survive?* New York: Sheed and Ward.

Bryk, Anthony S., Valerie E. Lee, and Peter B. Holland. 1993. *Catholic Schools and the Common Good*. Cambridge, MA: Harvard University Press.

Burke, Raymond, Archbishop. 2003. *On the Dignity of Human Life and Civic Responsibility: A Pastoral Letter to Christ's Faithful of the Diocese of La Crosse*. November 23. www.ewtn.com/library/BISHOPS/burkeciv.htm

———. 2004. "To Christ's Faithful of the Archdiocese of St. Louis: 'On Our Civic Responsibility for the Common Good.'" October 1. *St. Louis Review*. http://www.stlouisreview.com/abpcolumn.php?abpid=7051. Pp1–22.

Burns, Gene. 2005. *The Moral Veto: Framing Contraception, Abortion, and Pluralism in the United States*. New York: Cambridge University Press.

Carlin, David. 2003. *The Decline and Fall of the Catholic Church in America*. Manchester, N.H.: Sophia Institute Press.

Carville, James, Stanley Greenberg, and Bob Shrum. 2005. Reclaiming the White Catholic Vote. *Democracy Corps*, March 29, 17.

Casanova, José. 1994. *Public Religions in the Modern World*. Chicago: University of Chicago Press.

Castelli, Jim, and Joseph Gremillion. 1987. *The Emerging Parish: The Notre Dame Study of Catholic Life since Vatican II*. New York: Harper and Row.

Catechism of the Catholic Church. 1995. New York: Doubleday.

Center for Applied Research in the Apostolate. 2000. *National Parish Directory*. Washington, D.C.: Center for Applied Research in the Apostolate.

———. 2002. CARA Priest Poll. Washington, D.C.: Center for Applied Research in the Apostolate.

———. 2003. CARA Catholic Poll. Washington, D.C.: Center for Applied Research in the Apostolate.

Chapman, Tim. 2006. Boehner Letter on Rights of the Unborn. *Townhall Blogs, Capitol Report*. January 17. www.townhall.com

Coffey, Kathy. 1998. It's Time to End the Hypocrisy on Birth Control. *U.S. Catholic*, June, 24–25.

Cogley, John, and Rodger Van Allen. 1986. *Catholic America*. Kansas City, Mo.: Sheed and Ward.

Cohen, Steven M. 1983. *American Modernity and Jewish Identity*. New York: Tavistock.

Coleman, James S., Thomas Hoffer, and Sally Kilgore. 1982. *High School Achievement: Public, Catholic, and Private Schools Compared*. New York: Basic Books.

Colish, Marcia L. 2004. Reclaiming Our History: Belief and Practice in the Church. In *Governance, Accountability, and the Future of the Catholic Church*, edited by Francis Oakley and Bruce Russett. New York: Continuum.

Consortium of Social Science Associations. 2005. How Religious Beliefs Inform My Political Agenda. Presentation given by Rosa Delauro before the Officers of the Consortium of Social Science Associations, Washington, D.C., October 30.

D'Antonio, William V. 1966. The Layman in the Wake of Vatican II. *Ave Maria*, Lenten Series, 10–14.

———. 2005. "Catholic Voter Mobilization in the 2004 National Election." Paper delivered at the 37th World Congress of the International Institute of Sociology, Stockholm, Sweden, July 5–9, 12.

D'Antonio, William V., James D. Davidson, Dean R. Hoge, and Katherine Meyer. 2001. *American Catholics: Gender, Generation, and Commitment*. Lanham, Md.: AltaMira Press.

D'Antonio, William V., James D. Davidson, Dean R. Hoge, and Ruth A. Wallace. 1989. *American Catholic Laity in a Changing Church*. Kansas City, Mo.: Sheed and Ward.

———. 1996. *Laity American and Catholic: Transforming the Church*. Kansas City, Mo.: Sheed and Ward.

D'Antonio, William V., and Steven A. Tuch. 2004. Abortion Politics Revisited: Tweaking the Polarization Hypothesis. Unpublished manuscript. Washington, D.C.: Life Cycle Institute, Catholic University of America.

Davidson, James D. 2005. *Catholicism in Motion: The Church in American Society.* Liguori, Mo.: Liguori Publications.

Davidson, James D., and Dean R. Hoge. 2004. Catholics after the Scandal: A New Study's Major Findings. *Commonweal*, November 19, 13–17.

Davidson, James D., Thomas P. Walters, Bede Cisco, Katherine Meyer, and Charles E. Zech. 2003. *Lay Ministers and Their Spiritual Practices.* Huntington, Ind.: Our Sunday Visitor.

Davidson, James D., Andrea S. Williams, Richard A. Lamanna, Jan Stenftenagel, Kathleen Maas Weigert, William J. Whalen, and Patricia Wittberg. 1997. *The Search for Common Ground: What Unites and Divides Catholic Americans.* Huntington, Ind.: Our Sunday Visitor.

Delambo, David. 2005. *Lay Parish Ministers.* New York: National Pastoral Life Center.

DeLauro, Rosa. 2006. *Statement of Principles, Signed by Fifty-Five Catholic Democrats in the U.S. House of Representatives.* February 28. www.house.gov/delauro/press/2006/February/catholic_statement_2_8_06.html

DiIulio, John J., Jr. 2006. The Catholic Voter. *Commonweal*, March 24, 10–12.

Dillon, Michele. 1999. *Catholic Identity: Balancing Reason, Faith, and Power.* New York: Cambridge University Press.

Dolan, Jay P. 1985. *The American Catholic Experience: A History from Colonial Times to the Present.* New York: Doubleday Image.

———. 2002. *In Search of an American Catholicism.* New York: Oxford University Press.

Dulles, Avery, S.J. 1998. Orthodoxy and Social Change. *America*, June 20, 8–17.

Espinosa, Gastón, Vigilio Elizondo, and Jesse Miranda. 2003. Hispanic Churches in American Public Life: Summary of Findings. *Interim Reports* (paper series) 2003 (2). Notre Dame, Ind.: Institute for Latino Studies.

Fichter, Joseph Henry. 1951. *Southern Parish.* Chicago: University of Chicago Press.

———. 1954. *Social Relations in the Urban Parish.* Chicago: University of Chicago Press.

Filteau, Jerry. 2006. Cost of Clergy Sex Abuse Now Exceeds $1.5 Billion. *Catholic News Service.* March 31. www.catholicnews.com/data/stories/cns/0601876.htm

Finke, Roger, and Rodney Stark. 1992. *The Churching of America, 1776–1990.* New Brunswick, N.J.: Rutgers University Press.

———. 2000. *Acts of Faith: Explaining the Human Side of Religion.* Berkeley: University of California Press.

Finn, Daniel. 2005. Republicans and the Targeting of Religious Voters. *Commonweal*, November 4, 14–17.

Fleisher, Richard. 1993. Explaining the Change in Roll-Call Voting Behavior of Southern Democrats. *Journal of Politics* 55, no. 2: 327–41.

Fogarty, Gerald P., S.J. 2004. Episcopal Governance in the American Church. In *Governance, Accountability, and the Future of the Catholic Church.* edited by Francis Oakley and Bruce Russett. New York: Continuum.

Foundations and Donors Interested in Catholic Activities. 2005. Financial Accountability and Catholic Church Support: Findings of the 2005 Catholic Donor Attitude Survey. Washington, D.C.: Foundations and Donors Interested in Catholic Activities.

Fox, Thomas C. 1995. *Sexuality and Catholicism.* New York: Braziller.

Froehle, Bryan T., and Mary L. Gautier. 2000. *Catholicism USA: A Portrait of the Catholic Church in the United States.* Maryknoll, N.Y.: Orbis Books.

———. 2003. *Global Catholicism: Portrait of a World Church.* Maryknoll, N.Y.: Orbis Books.

Gallup, George, and Jim Castelli. 1987. *The American Catholic People: Their Beliefs, Practices and Values.* Garden City, N.Y.: Doubleday.

Gautier, Mary L., ed. 2005. *CARA Catholic Ministry Formation Directory.* Washington, D.C.: Center for Applied Research in the Apostolate.

Gautier, Mary L., and Mary E. Bendyna. 2006. *The Class of 2006: Survey of Ordinands to the Priesthood.* Washington, D.C.: Center for Applied Research in the Apostolate.

Gautier, Mary L., and Paul M. Perl. 2000. *National Parish Inventory.* Washington, D.C.: Center for Applied Research in the Apostolate.

Gibson, David. 2003. *The Coming Catholic Church: How the Faithful Are Shaping a New American Catholicism.* San Francisco: HarperSanFrancisco.

Gillis, Chester. 1999. *Roman Catholicism in America.* New York: Columbia University Press.

Glaeser, Edward L., Giacomo A. M. Ponzetto, and Jesse M. Shapiro. 2004. Strategic Extremism: Why Republicans and Democrats Divide on Religious Values. Discussion Paper No. 2044, October. Institute of Economic Research, Harvard University, 48.

Gleason, Phillip. 1994. American Catholicism and Liberalism. In *Catholicism and Liberalism,* edited by R. Bruce Douglass and David Hollenbach. Cambridge: Cambridge University Press.

Gray, Mark M. 2006. *Primary Trends, Challenges, and Outlook: A Special Report on U.S. Catholic Elementary Schools, 2000–2005.* Washington, D.C.: Center for Applied Research in the Apostolate.

Gray, Mark M., and Mary L. Gautier. 2004. *Understanding the Experience: A Profile of Lay Ecclesial Ministers Serving as Parish Life Coordinators.* Washington, D.C.: National Association for Lay Ministry.

———. 2006. *Primary Trends, Challenges, and Outlook: A Report on Catholic Elementary Schools.* Washington, D.C.: National Catholic Educational Association.

Gray, Mark M., and Paul M. Perl. 2006. Catholic Reactions to the News of Sexual Abuse Cases Involving Catholic Clergy. Working Paper No. 8. Washington, D.C.: Center for Applied Research in the Apostolate.

Greeley, Andrew M. 1973. *The New Agenda.* Garden City, N.Y.: Doubleday.

———. 1977. *The American Catholic: A Social Portrait.* New York: Basic Books.

———. 1979. *Crisis in the Church: A Study of Religion in America.* Chicago: Thomas More Press.

———. 1989. On the Margins of the Church: A Sociological Note. *America,* March 14, 194–98.

———. 1990. *The Catholic Myth.* New York: Scribner's.

———. 1999. *Furthermore: Memories of a Parish Priest.* New York: Tom Doherty Associates.

———. 2000. *The Catholic Imagination.* Berkeley: University of California Press.

———. 2004. *The Catholic Revolution.* Berkley: University of California Press.

Greeley, Andrew M., William C. McCready, and Kathleen McCourt. 1976. *Catholic Schools in a Declining Church*. Kansas City, Mo.: Sheed and Ward.

Greeley, Andrew M., and Peter H. Rossi. 1966. *The Education of Catholic Americans*. Chicago: Aldine.

Green, J. C., Corwin E. Smith, James L. Guth, and Lyman A. Kellstedt. 2004. The American Religious Landscape and the 2004 Presidential Vote: Increased Polarization. *Fourth National Survey of Religion and Politics, November–December 2004*. Akron, Ohio: University of Akron, 18.

Hetherington, Marc J. 2001. Resurgent Mass Partisanship: The Role of Elite Polarization. *American Political Science Review* 95, no. 3: 619–31.

Higham, John. 1988. *Strangers in the Land: Patterns of American Nativism, 1860–1925*. New York: Atheneum.

Hoge, Dean. 1987. *The Future of Catholic Leadership: Responses to the Priest Shortages*. Kansas City, Mo.: Sheed and Ward.

———. 2002. *The First Five Years of the Priesthood*. Collegeville, Minn.: Liturgical Press.

Hoge, Dean R., William D. Dinges, Mary Johnson, and Juan L. Gonzales Jr. 2001. *Young Adult Catholics: Religion in the Culture of Choice*. Notre Dame, Ind.: University of Notre Dame Press.

Hoge, Dean R., Benton Johnson, and Donald A. Luidens. 1994. *Vanishing Boundaries: The Religion of Mainline Protestant Baby Boomers*. Louisville, Ky.: Westminster/John Knox Press.

Hoge, Dean R., and Aniedi Okure. 2006. *International Priests in America: Challenges and Opportunities*. Collegeville, Minn.: Liturgical Press.

Hoge, Dean R., and Jacqueline E. Wenger. 2003. *Evolving Visions of the Priesthood*. Collegeville, Minn.: Liturgical Press.

Hunter, James Davison. 1991. *Culture Wars: The Struggle to Define America*. New York: Basic Books.

Jones, Melissa, and Joe Feuerherd. 2004. Meeting in Private, Bishops Leave Communion Decision to Local Leaders. *National Catholic Reporter*, July 2, 26.

Kelly, George A. 1959. *The Catholic Family Handbook*. New York: Random House.

Kennedy, Eugene. 1988. *Tomorrow's Catholics, Yesterday's Church*. San Francisco: Harper and Row.

Langer, Gary, and Jon Cohen. 2005. Voters and Values in the 2004 Election. *Public Opinion Quarterly* 69, no. 5: 744–59.

Layman, Geoffrey C., and Thomas M. Carsey. 2002. Party Polarization and "Conflict Extension" in the American Electorate. *American Journal of Political Science* 46, no. 4: 786–802.

Lee, Bernard J., with William V. D'Antonio. 2000. *The Catholic Experience of Small Christian Communities*. Mahwah, N.J.: Paulist Press.

Leege, David C., et al. 2002. *The Politics of Cultural Differences*. Princeton, N.J.: Princeton University Press.

Lenski, Gerhard. 1961. *The Religious Factor: A Sociological Study of Religion's Impact on Politics, Economics, and Family Life*. Garden City, N.Y.: Doubleday.

Lieberg, Elissa. 2005. Primacy of Conscience. *Commonweal*, November 4, 26.

Los Angeles Times. 1987, August 14–19. Research Report on 1987 Nationwide Poll #128.

Massa, Mark. 2001. *Anti-Catholicism in America: The Last Acceptable Prejudice.* New York: Crossroad.

McClory, Robert. 1995. *Turning Point.* New York: Crossroad.

McCloskey, John. 2006. State of US Catholic Church at Beginning of 2006. *Spero News.* January 16. www.speroforum.com/site/article.asp?idCategory = 34&idsub = 127&id = 24

McGreevy, John T. 1996. *Parish Boundaries: The Catholic Encounter with Race in the Twentieth-Century Urban North.* Chicago: University of Chicago Press.

Mehlman, Ken. 2003, January 23. Statement Made to Honor the Catholic March on Washington to Celebrate Pro-Life Day. Washington, D.C.: Republican National Committee.

Miller, Donald E. 1997. *Reinventing American Protestantism.* Berkeley: University of California Press.

Morris, Charles. 1997. *American Catholics: The Saints and Sinners Who Built America's Most Powerful Church.* New York: Times Books.

Murray, John Courtney. 1960. *We Hold These Truths: Catholic Reflections on the American Proposition.* New York: Sheed and Ward.

New York Times. 1960. R. F. Kennedy's Part in King Case Scored. October 12, 12.

New York Times. 2004, June 5. Bush Meets Pope, Who Voices His Displeasure over Iraq.

Niemi, Richard, and Michael Hanmer. 2004. *College Students in the 2004 Election. Fact Sheet.* College Park: University of Maryland School of Public Policy.

Noonan, John T. 2005. *A Church That Cannot Change: The Development of Catholic Moral Teaching.* Notre Dame, Ind.: University of Notre Dame Press.

Oakley, Francis, and Bruce Russett, eds. 2004. *Governance, Accountability, and the Future of the Catholic Church.* New York: Continuum.

Perl, Paul M., Jennifer Z. Greely, and Mark M. Gray. 2004. How Many Hispanics Are Catholic? A Review of Survey Data and Methodology. Washington, D.C.: Center for Applied Research in the Apostolate. http://cara.georgetown.edu/ Hispanic Catholics.pdf

Perlmutter, Philip. 1999. *Legacy of Hate: A Short History of Ethnic, Religious, and Racial Prejudice in America.* Armonk, N.Y.: M. E. Sharpe.

Pew Research Center. 2005. Religion and Public Life: A Faith-Based Partisan Divide. In *Trends 2005.* Washington, D.C.: Pew Research Center. http://pewresearch.org/ assets/files/trends2005.pdf

Pew Research Center. 2006. Is There a Culture War? *Event Transcript.* May 23. http:// pewforum.org/events/index.php?EventID = 112

Philibert, Paul J. 2004. *Stewards of God's Mysteries: Priestly Spirituality in a Changing Church.* Collegeville, Minn.: Liturgical Press.

Poloma, Margaret M. 2005. Charisma and Structure in the Assemblies of God: Revisiting O'Dea's Five Dilemmas. In *Church, Identity, and Change: Theology and Denominational Structures in Unsettled Times,* edited by David A. Roozen and James R. Nieman. Grand Rapids, Mich.: Eerdmans.

Putnam, Robert D. 2000. *Bowling Along: The Collapse and Revival of American Community.* New York: Simon and Schuster.

Pyle, Ralph E. 2006. Trends in Religious Stratification: Have Religious Group Socio-

Economic Distinctions Declined in Recent Decades? *Sociology of Religion* 67, no. 1: 61–79.

Rexhausen, Jeff, Michael Cieslak, Mary L. Gautier, and Robert J. Miller. 2004. *A National Study of Recent Diocesan Efforts at Parish Reorganization in the United States: Pathways for the Church of the 21st Century*. Dubuque, Iowa: Loras College Press.

Rosenberg, Morris. 1979. *Conceiving the Self*. New York: Basic Books.

Stark, Rodney, and Charles Y. Glock. 1968. *Patterns of Religious Commitment*. Berkeley: University of California Press.

Steinfels, Peter. 2003. *A People Adrift: The Crisis of the Roman Catholic Church in America*. New York: Simon and Schuster.

Stryker, Sheldon. 1991. Identity Theory. In *Encyclopedia of Sociology*, vol. 2, edited by Edgar F. Borgatta and Marie L. Borgatta. New York: Macmillan.

Stryker, Sheldon, and Richard T. Serpe. 1994. Identity Salience and Psychological Centrality: Equivalent, Overlapping, or Complementary Concepts? *Social Psychological Quarterly* 57: 16–35.

United States Conference of Catholic Bishops. 2005a. Co-workers in the Vineyard of the Lord. Washington, D.C.: USCCB Publishing.

———. 2005. *Renewing Our Commitment to Catholic Elementary and Secondary Schools in the Third Millennium*. Washington, D.C.: USCCB Publishing.

———. 2006. *Statement on Responsibilities of Catholics in Public Life*. Washington, D.C.: USCCB Office of Media Relations, March 10.

U.S. Census Bureau. 2006. Annual Estimates of the Population by Sex, Race and Hispanic or Latino Origin for the United States: April 1, 2000 to July 1, 2005 (NC-EST2005-03), table 3. Washington, D.C.: U.S. Census Bureau, Population Division. www.census.gov/popest/national/asrh/NC-EST2005-srh.html

USA Today. 1993, August 10. How U.S. Catholics View Their Church. Based on a *USA Today*/CNN/Gallup Poll.

Van Biema, David. 2004. Does Abortion Trump All Other Issues? *Time*, June 21, 37.

Varacalli, Joseph. 2000. *Bright Promise, Failed Community: Catholics and the American Public Order*. Lanham, Md.: Lexington Books.

Wallace, Ruth A. 1992. *They Call Her Pastor*. Albany: State University of New York Press.

———. 2003. *They Call Him Pastor: Married Men in Charge of Catholic Parishes*. Mahwah, N.J.: Paulist Press.

Washington Post. 1960. Negro Group Raps King's Support of Kennedy. November 2.

Weber, Max. 1947. *The Theory of Social and Economic Organization*. Glencoe, Ill.: Free Press.

White, John K., and William V. D'Antonio. 2007. "Catholics and the Politics of Change: The Presidential Campaigns of Two JFKs." In *Religion and the Bush Presidency*, edited by Mark J. Rozell and Gleaves Whitney. New York: Palgrave/Macmillan.

Wills, Garry. 2000. *Papal Sin: Structures of Deceit*. New York: Doubleday.

Yamane, David. 2005. *The Catholic Church in State Politics: Negotiating Prophetic Demands and Political Realities*. Lanham, Md.: Rowman & Littlefield.

Zogby, John. 2005. 2004 Presidential Election. Report, February 7. Washington, D.C.: Zogby International.

Index

About the Authors

William V. D'Antonio (Ph.D. 1958, Michigan State University) is a fellow at the Life Cycle Institute, Catholic University in Washington, D.C. Before coming to Catholic University in 1993, D'Antonio taught sociology at Michigan State, Notre Dame, and the University of Connecticut, and chaired the departments at Notre Dame and Connecticut. From 1982 to 1991 he served as executive officer of the American Sociological Association in Washington, D.C. He is coauthor of eight books, and coeditor of four others, covering the fields of family, religion, politics, and introductory sociology.

James D. Davidson (Ph.D., University of Notre Dame) is professor of sociology at Purdue University. He specializes in the sociology of religion, with particular emphasis on studies of religious stratification and American Catholicism. He is author, or coauthor, of *Catholicism in Motion* (Liguori Publications, 2005), *Lay Ministers and Their Spiritual Practices* (Our Sunday Visitor, 2003), *American Catholics* (AltaMira, 2001), *The Search for Common Ground* (Our Sunday Visitor, 1997), *Laity: American and Catholic* (Sheed and Ward, 1996), and *American Catholic Laity in a Changing Church* (Sheed and Ward, 1989). *The Search for Common Ground* received the 1998 Research Award from the National Conference for Catechetical Leadership. Dr. Davidson has also published recent articles in *America*, *Commonweal*, and *Liguorian*. He is the current president of the Association for the Sociology of Religion. He also has been president of the Religious Research Association and the North Central Sociological Association, editor of the *Review of Religious Research*, and executive officer of the Society for the Scientific Study of Religion. He has won his department's Excellence in Teaching Award and Indiana's Community Service Award.

Dean R. Hoge (Ph.D. 1970, Harvard) is professor of sociology emeritus and fellow of the Life Cycle Institute at Catholic University of America in Washington, D.C. He has spent three decades researching American religion, social trends, and youth, producing seventeen books and one hundred articles, many coauthored. His book *Vanishing Boundaries*, coauthored with Benton Johnson and Donald Luidens, won the SSSR Distinguished Book Award in 1994. His recent books include *The First Five Years of the Priesthood* (2002); *Evolving Visions of the Priesthood* (coauthored, 2003); *Pastors in Transition: Why Clergy Leave Local Church Ministry* (coauthored, 2005); *International Priests in America* (coauthored, 2006); *Experiences of Priests Ordained Five to Nine Years* (2006); and *Religion and the New Immigrants* (coauthored, 2007). He is past president of the Religious Research Association, and current president-elect of the Society for the Scientific Study of Religion.

Mary L. Gautier (Ph.D. 1995, Louisiana State University) is a senior research associate at the Center for Applied Research in the Apostolate (CARA) at Georgetown University in Washington, D.C. Before coming to CARA in June 1998, Dr. Gautier taught sociology at Louisiana State University and at Texas Christian University in Fort Worth, Texas, and served as a lay pastoral associate at a parish in Baton Rouge, Louisiana, for six years. At CARA, Dr. Gautier specializes in Catholic demographic trends in the United States, manages CARA databases on Church information, and conducts demographic projects and computer-aided mapping. She also edits *The CARA Report*, a quarterly research newsletter, and other CARA publications. She is coauthor of two books on Catholicism published by Orbis Books.